GRACE AND GLORY

Sermons Preached in the Chapel

—OF—

Princeton Theological Seminary

&

THE IDEA OF BIBLICAL THEOLOGY AS A SCIENCE AND AS A THEOLOGICAL DISCIPLINE

Inaugural Address at
Princeton Theological Seminary

GEERHARDUS VOS

ANTHEM PUBLISHING

A Division of re:SOURCE DIGITAL PUBLISHING

Formatted and Printed in the United States of America

Digital edition also available.

ISBN: 9798697877425

ANTHEM PUBLISHING

GRACE AND GLORY

Sermons Preached in the Chapel

—OF—

Princeton Theological Seminary

&

THE IDEA OF BIBLICAL THEOLOGY AS A SCIENCE AND AS A THEOLOGICAL DISCIPLINE

Inaugural Address at
Princeton Theological Seminary

GEERHARDUS VOS

I. THE WONDERFUL TREE

Hosea 14:8

"I am like a green fir tree; from me is thy fruit found."

This prophetic utterance represents one of the two inseparable sides in the makeup of religion. If we say that religion consists of what God is for man, and of what man is for God, then our text in the divine statement, "From me is thy fruit found," stands for the former. To balance it with the other side some such word as that of Isaiah might be taken, "The vineyard of Jehovah of Hosts is the house of Israel." Nor would it be an arbitrary combination of disconnected passages thus pointedly to place the one over against the other. In each case a careful study of the prophet would reveal that not some incidental turn of thought, but an habitual point of view, imparting tone and color to the entire religious experience, had found expression in a characteristic form of statement. The two points of view are supplementary, and, taken together, exhaustive of what the normal relation between God and man involves. Until we learn to unite the Isaiah-type of piety with that of Hosea, we shall not attain a full and harmonious development of our religious life.

Let us this time look at the half-circle of truth expressed by the older prophet. The Text stands in the most beautiful surroundings, not merely within Hosea's own prophecy, but in the entire Old Testament. There is a charm about this chapter more easily felt than described. It is like the clear shining after rain, when the sun riseth, a morning without clouds. In what precedes there is much that is hard to understand. Hosea's style is abrupt, full of strange leaps from vision to vision. But Here We suddenly pass out of the labyrinth of involved oracles into the clear open. It is a prophecy suffused with deep feeling. All the native tenderness of the prophet, the acute sensitiveness, and responsiveness of his emotional nature, rendering him, as it were, a musical instrument expectant of the Spirit's touch, are here in striking evidence; the dissonances of the many prophecies of woe resolve themselves in the sweet harmony of a closing prophecy of promise. And besides, the incomparable light of the future shines upon this chapter. It Is Bathed In the glory of the latter days, those glories which no prophet could describe without giving forth the finest notes of which his organ was capable. In the repertoire of the prophets the choicest always belongs to the farthest. When Their Eye rests on the world to come, a miracle is wrought in their speech, so that, in accord with the things described, it borrows from the melodies of the other world.

Still the spell thrown upon our minds by this piece is by no means wholly, or even chiefly, due to its form. It is the peculiar content that captivates the heart as the music captivates the ear. It is not to be expected of any prophet that he shall put into his prophecies relating to the end indiscriminately of his treasure, but chiefly what is to him its most precious part, that which the Spirit of revelation had led him, and him above others, to apprehend and appreciate. From Utterances of this kind, therefore, we get our best perception of what lay nearest to the prophet's heart. So, certainly, it is here with Hosea. In its last analysis, the charm of this chapter is none other than the innate charm of the prophet's most cherished acquaintance with Jehovah. And, applied to the future, this may be summed up in the idea that the possession of Jehovah Himself by his people will be of all the delights of the world to come the chief and most satisfying, the paradise within the paradise of God. The whole description leads up to this and revolves around it. As preparing for it, the return to Jehovah is mentioned first.

The end of the great change is that the people may once more live in the presence of God. The prayer the prophet puts upon their lips is, "Take away all iniquity," with the emphasis upon the all, so as to indicate that not x) otherwise than by the absolute removal of all sin can the cloudless atmosphere be created for the supreme enjoyment of God. And the people pledge that their eyes and hearts henceforth shall be closed to the lure of idols. As a helpless orphan Israel casts herself upon Jehovah's grace: "We will not say anymore to the work of our hands, ye are our gods, for in Thee the fatherless findeth mercy." But clearest of all the idea appears in the direct speech Jehovah is represented as in that day addressing the people, to the effect that He Himself is eagerly desirous to pour out the riches of his affection upon the heart of Israel and meet her desire for Him to the utmost measure of its capacity: "I have answered and will regard him; I will be as the dew to Israel: he shall blossom as the lily, and cast forth his roots as Lebanon. His Branches Shall Spread, and his beauty shall be as the olive tree, and his smell as Lebanon. They shall revive as the grain, and blossom as the vine; I am like a green fir tree; from me is thy fruit found." It will be seen from this that our text is really the climax of this speech of Jehovah. Through the addition of image to image the divine purpose of giving Himself gathers intensity, till at last God appears as a green tree, bearing fruit for his people. This is truly a marvelous representation, well adapted to startle us, when we think ourselves into it. It seems to imply something in God that, in the desire for self-communication exceeds even the strongest affection of a human parent for his children. And yet, my hearers, when reflecting upon it for a moment, can we fail to observe that the marvel in it is nothing else than the heart-miracle of all true religion, the great paradox underlying all God's concern with us. That He, the all-sufficient One, forever rich and blessed in Himself, should, as it were, take Himself in His own hands, making of Himself an object to be bestowed upon a creature, so as to change before the eyes of the prophet into a tree, showering its fruit upon Israel, lavish as nothing in all nature but a tree can be, this surely is something to be wondered at, and something which, though it recurs a thousand times, no experience or enjoyment ought to be able to rob of its wonder. There is in it more than we convey by the term "communion with God." That admits of relativity, there are degrees in it, but this figure depicts the thing in its highest and deepest possibility, as flowing from the divine desire so to take us into the immediate, intimate circle of his own life and blessedness, as to make all its resources serve our delight, a river of pleasures from his right hand. It might almost seem as if there were here a reversal of the process of religion itself, inasmuch as God appears putting Himself at the service of man, and that with the absolute generosity born of supreme love. This relation into which it pleases God to receive Israel with Himself has in it a sublime abandon it knows neither restraint nor reserve. Using human language one might say that God enters into this heart and soul and mind and strength. Since God thus gives Himself to his people for fruition, and his resources are infinite, there is no possibility of their ever craving more or seeking more of Him than it is good for them to receive. To deprive religion of this, by putting it upon the barren basis of pure disinterestedness, is not merely a pretense to be wiser than God; it is also an act of robbing God of His own joy through refusing the joy into which He has, as it were, resolved Himself for us. So far from being a matter of gloom and depression, religion in its true concept is an exultant state, the supreme feast and sabbath of the soul. Of course, in saying this, we do not forget that such religion in its absoluteness can be for a fallen race but a memory and a hope. The painful and distressing elements that enter into our Christian experience are by no means the product of a perverted and bigoted imagination. Religion need not be in error or insincere when it makes man put ashes on his head, instead of every day anointing his countenance with the oil of gladness. In order to be of any use whatever to us in a state of sin it must assume the form of redemption, and from redemption the elements of penitence and pain are inseparable. Here lies the one source of all the discomfort and self-repression entering into the occupation of man with God, of the sad litany which revealed religion, and to some extent even natural religion, has chanted through the ages. Let no one in a spirit of superficial light-heartedness ridicule it, for, though it may have its excrescences and hypocrisies, in itself it is as inevitable as the joy of religion itself. There is as much reason to pity the man to whom religion has brought no sorrow as the one to whom it has brought no joy. The bitter herbs may not be omitted from the Paschal feast of deliverance. Perhaps The saddest thing to be said of sin is that it has thus been able to invade religion at its very core of joy, injecting into it the opposite of its nature. And yet it is equally true that there is no religious joy like the joy engendered by redemption. Nor is this simply due to the law of contrast which makes the relief of deliverance proportionate to the pain which it succeeds. A more particular cause is at work here. In redemption God opens up Himself to us and surrenders his inner life to our possession in a wholly unprecedented manner of which the religion of nature can have neither dream nor anticipation. It is more clearly in saving us than in creating us that God shows Himself God. To taste and feel the riches of his Godhead, as freely given unto us, one must have passed not only through the abjectness and poverty and despair of sin but through the overwhelming experience of salvation. He who is saved explores and receives more of God than unfallen man or even the unfallen angels can. The song of

Moses and of the Lamb has in it a deeper exultation than that which the sons of God and the morning stars sang together for joy in the Creator. This redemptive self-communication of God is what the prophet has particularly in mind in recording the promise or text. As already stated, it is a gift of the future, and, of course, the entire future stands to him, as to every prophet, in the sign of redemption. Not as if the future meant only redemption. There Is No more characteristic trait in prophecy than that it never makes the crisis of judgment a road to mere restoration of what existed before, but the occasion for the bringing in of something wholly new and inexperienced in the past, so that Jehovah comes out of the conflict, not as one who has barely snatched his work from destruction, but as the great Victor who has made the forces of sin and evil his servants for the accomplishment of a higher and wider purpose. There is an exact correspondence in this respect between the large movement of redemption, taken as a whole, and the enactment of its principles on a smaller scale within the history of Israel. As the second Adam is greater than the first, and the paradise of the future fairer than that of the

past, so the new-born Israel to the prophet's vision is a
nobler figure and exists under far more favorable conditions
than the empirical Israel of before. Once its Peniel-night is
over, it will live in the light and feed upon the goodness of
God, and be beautified through its religious embrace of
Him. This thought is not unclearly suggested by the very
figure of our text. Whatever may be the precise tree species
designated by the word "*berosh*," here rendered as fir tree, at
any rate an evergreen is meant, a tree retaining its verdure
in all seasons of the year, never failing in its power to shade
and to refresh. There a son is none other than that for which
in vs. 6 Israel in its beauty is compared to the olive tree, a
tree likewise perennially clothed with foliage. But there is
still something else and far more wonderful about this tree.
While by nature not a fruit-bearing tree in the ordinary
sense, it changes itself into One before the eyes of the
prophet. If nothing more than the idea of fruitfulness were
intended, the figure of the olive tree would have lain closer
at hand. But the labor of the olive is a process of nature and
bound to the seasons, and evidently what Hosea wishes to
express is the concurrence in the same tree of miraculous

fruitage, perennial yield, and never-failing shade, for the context emphasizes all three. It is evident that we are here in another tree-world than that of Palestine; it is the neighborhood of the tree of life of which we read elsewhere that it yields its fruit every month. Plainly Jehovah is thus represented on account of his specific redemptive productiveness, and that in its heightened future form, when new unheard of influences shall proceed from Him for the nourishing and enjoyment of his people. Surely here is something that nature, even God's goodness in nature, could never yield. Perhaps we are not assuming too much by finding still another element in the comparison. In emphasizing the verdant, living character of Jehovah with reference to Israel, the prophet may have had in mind, by way of contrast, the pagan deity from which these qualities of life and fruitfulness and miraculous provision are utterly absent. There used to stand beside the altar of idolatry a pole rudely fashioned in the image of Asherah, the spouse of Baal and goddess of fruitfulness. Nothing could have more strikingly symbolized the barrenness and hopelessness of nature worship than this dead stump in which no bud could sprout, and on which no bird would alight, and of which no fruit was to be found forever. How desperate is the plight of those Canaanites, modern no less than ancient, who must look for the satisfaction of their hunger to the dead wood of the Asherah of nature, because they have no faith in the perpetual miracle of the fruit-bearing fir tree of redemption.

But let us endeavor to ascertain what concrete meaning the prophet attaches to the image of the text. What is the fruit that is promised to Israel? To answer this we shall have to go beyond the confines of the text and look around us in the preceding prophecy. The study of this will teach that there are four outstanding features to Jehovah's gift to Israel of the fruition of Himself. We find that it is eminently personal, exclusive, individual, and transforming in its influence. In the first place, then, Israel's fruition of Jehovah is eminently personal. One might truthfully say that the idea of the possession of one's God in this pointedly personal sense is an idea grown on the soil of revelation, nurtured by the age-long self-communication of God to his own. To be sure, the thought that the fortunes of life must be related to the deity is a common one in Semitic religion. Edom and

Moab and Ammon also have joy before their gods. But this is still something far different from having joy in one's God. The latter is Israel's distinction. To have a god and to have God are two things. The difference can be measured by the presence and the absence of the covenant idea in the two different circles. When Jehovah, entering into covenant with Israel says, "I will be unto you a God, and ye shall be unto me a people," this means infinitely more than the trite idea: henceforth ye shall worship me and I will cultivate you. It is the mutual surrender of person to person. Jehovah throws in his lot with Israel, no less truly than Israel's lot is bound up with Jehovah. To express it in terms of the text one would have to force the figure and say that not merely the fruit, nor merely the tree for its fruit, but the tree itself, as a glorious living being, is the cherished treasure of the owner. The sense of this is so vivid that it has given rise to the phrase "Portion of Israel" as a personal name of God. To the mind of Hosea the most forcible, indeed final and absolute, expression of this precious truth had been reached in the form of the marriage-union between God and Israel. That is simply a closer specification of the covenant idea, and it brings out precisely that side of it on which we are dwelling, the personal aspect of the union involved. While this is from the nature of the case conceived of as mutual, yet the emphasis rests perceptibly on the divine side of it. To be sure, Israel also personally surrendered herself to Jehovah, for we read that she made answer in the days of her youth, and through Jeremiah God declares: "I remember thee for the kindness of thy youth, the love of thine espousals, how thou wentest after me in the wilderness, in a land that was not sown." But that was in the beginning; in the sequel Israel soon proved indifferent and faithless. The burden of the message lies in the ascription of this to Jehovah as a permanent, unchangeable disposition. He had not for one moment ceased to be the person a land intimate life companion of Israel. The covenant might be suspended, but so long as it lasted, it could have no other meaning than this, for this lay at its heart. In a number of delicate little touches the prophet reveals his consciousness of it. After the dire calamities of the judgment have overwhelmed the people and seemingly left nothing further to be swept away, then, as a climax, by the side of which all else shrinks into insignificance, Jehovah announces that He will now personally withdraw from Israel. And corresponding to this, after they have sat many days in the desolation of exile, all but divorced from God, the first and supremely important step in their conversion is that they come trembling unto Jehovah and unto his goodliness in the latter days. Even in the Messianic outlook this strongly personal view point appears. With a peculiarly affectionate turn to the thought the prophet represents the people as in the end seeking David their king, through remembrance of the sure covenant mercies attaching to the name of one who was the man after God's heart, and thus in himself a pledge of the divine love towards the people. In the sphere of external, terrestrial gifts the same principle applies. Here, of course, revealed religion comes nearest to the circle of ideas of paganism. Baal, no less than Jehovah, is supposed to give to his servants the produce of the soil. But what a principle difference between the attitude in which paganism entertains this idea and the spirit in which the prophet expects Israel to cherish it! The pagan cult cleaves to the sod, and buries itself in the heaps of grain and the rivers of oil, and remembers not, except in the most external way, the god who gave. The worship sits loosely upon the life; it is a habit rather than an organic function, and subject to change, if the turn of fortune requires. Paganized Israel herself is introduced as speaking in the distress of harvest failure, "I will go after my lovers, that give me my bread and my water, my wool and my flax, mine oil and my drink." "But," says Jehovah, "she knew not that I gave her the grain and the must and the oil and multiplied unto her silver and gold." To Hosea the main principle is that the gifts shall come to the people with the dew of Jehovah's love upon them, deriving their value not so much from what they are intrinsically but from the fact of their being tokens of affection, to each one of which clings something of the personality of the giver. And Jehovah knows such a special art of putting Himself into these favors; He is not imprisoned in them as are the Baals, but freely lives in and loves through them, so as to make them touch the heart of Israel. When the time of her new betrothal comes, and she sees the gifts for her adornment, she exclaims, "Ishi, my husband!" and no longer "Baali, my lord!" Notice the role that nature plays in effecting this; the externals are by no means despised; they have simply ceased to be externals, and been turned into one great sacramental vehicle of spiritual favor. Jehovah sets in motion the whole circuit of nature for the service of his people: "It shall come to pass in that day, I will answer the heavens and they shall answer the earth, and the earth shall answer the grain and the new wine and the oil, and they shall answer Jezreel." The things do not mutely grow, they speak, they answer, they sing, and the voice that travels through them is the voice of Jehovah. Nature becomes the instrument of grace. That in the spiritual sphere proper everything proceeds along the same line need hardly be pointed out. God speaks comfortably unto Israel to call her back to repentance. He loves her freely, and it is through making her realize this fact that He effects her return. His bridal gifts to Israel are righteousness and mercy and faithfulness and loving kindness. The mercy that He shows them in their distress is at bottom something far deeper and finer and more spiritualized than the generic sense of pity. It is *chesed*, loving-kindness, that is, mercy intensified a thousand times by the tenderness of an antecedent love. It is not compassion that saves Israel, for compassion, though truly spiritual in itself, lies but on the circumference of that mysterious saving movement that springs in the divine heart from love and grace as its center.

In the second place the possession and enjoyment for which Jehovah offers Himself to Israel are an exclusive relationship. Here the figure of marriage comes into play. Hosea has greatly idealized this figure, at least as compared with the customs of his time. No matter which side we choose in the exegetical dispute as to whether the first three chapters are allegory or recite facts, in either case, be it by a unique experience or through a unique vision, the prophet has produced a marriage ideal fit to be the parable of the covenant. In this idealized form it renders most faithfully the latter's essential features. For emphasizing the pure spirituality of the relation nothing could be more suitable. In this respect it excels even the figure of fatherhood and sonship. For these originate in nature without free choice. The bond of marriage, as conceived by Hosea, was established through a spiritual process. God, after having created Israel, sought and cultivated her affection. He did this in the beginning and will do it again in the future. So intent is the prophet upon guarding the ideal, ethereal perfection of the union that he studiously avoids representing the coming state of blessedness as a restoration of the previous bond, lest the sin-clouds of the past should project their shadows into it. Therefore the consistency of the figure is disregarded no reparation, no remarriage is mentioned; the past is blotted out; the sin loses both stain and sting; the future arises as a fresh creation out of the waters of oblivion beneath which Israel's guilt has been buried. It is the new, otherwise unrepeatable, love of the first bloom of youth shedding its fragrance overall: "I will betroth thee unto me in faithfulness, and I will say, Thou art my people, and they shall say, Thou art our God." Now this same idealization also appears in regard to the mutual exclusiveness of the covenant attachment. For we must remember that the prophet affirms this with equal absoluteness with reference to the covenant husband as to the wife, and in this respect custom in his day fell far short of the ideal. When God gives Himself to Israel it is with the clear understanding and promise that He does not do so to any other people. And the exclusiveness on the part of God demands an equally exclusive return of love and service such as shall leave no room for strange devotion. Still at this point the reality somehow again transcends the figure. Not that God is husband, but the kind of husband He is, comes under consideration. It is not merely his general honor that is at stake, as would be the case in ordinary human marriage; apart from all else the specifically divine character of his Person and love renders exclusiveness imperative. Even in giving Himself God remains God and requires from Israel the acknowledgment of this. The gift Is divine and desires for itself a temple where no other presence shall be tolerated. If we feel God to be ours, then we also feel that no one but God can ever be ours in the same exclusive ineffable sense and that every similar absorption by any purely human relationship would partake of the idolatrous. The only thing that can give a faint suggestion of the engrossing character of the divine hold upon His people is the first awakening of what we call romantic love in the youthful heart with its concentration of all the intensified impulses and forces and desires upon one object and its utter obliviousness to all other interests. This actually in some measure resembles the single-minded, world-forgetful affection we owe to God, and for that very reason is called worship. But it is a state of momentary, supernormal exaltation, which cannot last, because in the creature there is not that which will justify and sustain it. Eternalize this and put into it the divine instead of the human, and you will have a dim image of what the mutual exclusiveness of devotion between God and man in the covenant bond implies. Here lies the infallible test of what is truly religious in our so-called religion. Everything that lacks the unique reference to God, as its supreme owner and end, is automatically ruled out from that sphere. Yea, anything that is cherished and cultivated apart from God in such a sense that we cannot carry it with us in the Godward movement of our life, becomes necessarily a hindrance, a profanation, and at last a source of idolatry. Man's nature is so built that he must be religious either in a good or in a bad sense. Ill-religious he may, but simply non-religious he cannot be. What he fails to bring into the Temple of God, he is sure to set up on the outside, and not seldom at the very gate, as a rival object of worship. And often the more ostensibly spiritual and refined these things are, the more potent and treacherous the lure. The Modern man who seeks to save and perfect himself has a whole pantheon of ideals, each of them a veritable god sapping the vitals of his religion. Nay, the prophet goes even farther than this: Jehovah Himself can be made an object of idolatry. If one fails to form a true conception of his character and weaves into the mental image formed of Him the false features gathered from other quasi-divine beings, then, whatever the name employed, be it God or Jehovah or even "the Father," the reality of the divine life is not in it. In such a case it is the perverted image that evokes the worship, instead of the true God. Hence the prophet does not hesitate to place the calf of Bethel, in which all Israel meant to serve Jehovah, on a line with the idols of the Canaanites, and to call it outright by the name of Baal. This may remind us that the rival interest which interferes with the exclusiveness of our devotion to God is not seldom taken from the sphere of religion itself. Where that happens, the most insidious form of adultery ensues, because it permits the delusion to remain that with an undivided heart we are cleaving to the Lord. Our outgoing activities, or good works of service, our concern with the externals of religion, all this, unless kept in the closest, most vital contact with God Himself, will inevitably tend to acquire a degree of detachment and independence in which it may easily withdraw from God the consecration that ought to go to and the satisfaction that ought to come from Him alone. There is even such a thing as worshipping one's religion instead of one's God. How easily the mind falls into the habit of merely enlisting God as an ally in the fight for creature-betterment, almost oblivious to the fact that He is the King of glory for whose sake the whole world exists and the entire battle is waged! Sometimes it is difficult not to feel that God is reckoned with, chiefly because his name and prestige and resources are indispensable for success in a cause that really transcends Him, and that the time may yet come when as a supernumerary he will be set aside. Is it not precisely this that often makes the atmosphere of Christian work so chill and uninspiring? Though we compel the feet to move to the accelerated pace of our modern religious machinery, the heart is atrophied and the lukewarm blood flows sluggishly through our veins. Let each one examine himself whether to any extent he is caught in the whirl of this centrifugal movement. The question, though searching, is an extremely simple one: Do we love God for his own sake, and find in this love the inspiration of service, or do we patronize Him as an influential partner under whose auspices we can better conduct our manifold activities in the service of the world ? It was not said with a manward reference alone, that if one should bestow all his goods to feed the poor, and give his body to be burned, and not have love, it would profit him nothing. That which is necessary to allow an act towards our neighbor must be certainly indispensable in any service for rendering it sacrifice well-pleasing unto God.

In the third place the fruition of Himself granted by God to us is individual. There can be no division to it; each must of necessity receive the whole, if he is to receive it at all. This follows from the nature of the gift itself. If the gift consisted of impersonal values, either material or spiritual, the supply might be quantitatively distributed over many persons. But being, as it is, the personal favor of God, it must be poured as a whole into the receptacle of the human heart. The parable of marriage not only teaches that the covenant relation is a monogamic one, but implies besides that it is a bond binding unitary soul to soul. There is a sinner sanctuary of communion, where all else disappears from sight, and the believer shut in with God gazes upon his loveliness, and appropriates Him, as though outside of Him nothing mattered or existed. These may be fugitive moments, and they may be rare in our experience, but we surely must know them, if God's fruit-bearing for us is to be a reality in our lives. The prophet evidently had a feeling for this, although the dispensation of the covenant under which he lived made it far more difficult to attain than in our time. The collective method of procedure pursued at that stage related everything in the first instance to the nation of Israel. To it belong the election, the love, the union with God, the future. It is quite in accordance with this that Israel as a body appears as the bride and wife of Jehovah, or in the terms of a different figure as the son He has called out of Egypt. Nonetheless it yields a pure abstraction, when this is carried to the extreme of a denial of every individual bond between the single Israelite and Jehovah. On the basis of the collective relationship, in which the many unite as one, there must of necessity have sprung up an individual attachment, in which the single believer and Jehovah directly touched each other. As there was private sacrifice alongside of the public ritual service, so there must have flourished personal worship and affection for God in the hearts of the pious. The devotional fragrance wafted to us from so many a page in the Old Testament bears abundant witness to this. But, while no true Israelite could be entirely without this, there existed doubtless many degrees in the individualizing of what was so largely a common possession. The nature of the prophetic office brought with it a certain detachment from the mass and a peculiar intimacy with Jehovah. And yet the note of individualism is not equally strong in all the prophets. It is interesting to observe where and when and how it emerges. Its two great exponents before the exile are Hosea and Jeremiah. These two speak not only from and for Jehovah but also to Jehovah. They are preeminently the prophets of prayer. In the case of each there appears to be some connection between the temperament of the prophet and the cultivation of this element. Both exceptionally endowed in their emotional nature, they instinctively sought, and under the influence of the Spirit were enabled to find, what could satisfy this deep instinct. Religion as centered in the heart cannot but incline towards individualism, for the heart with its hidden feelings is the most incapable of duplication of all the factors that enter into it. Belief and intent of will may be standardized; the emotional reaction is like the wind of heaven: we hear the sound thereof, yet know not whence it cometh nor whither it goeth; so it is with the world of religious feeling; it has a coloring and tone of its own in each individual child of God. Hosea being of a most tender and impressionable temperament was on that account chosen to secure for the covenant-bond in his own life, and through his influence in the life of others, that sweet privacy and inwardness which forms the most precious possession of every pious soul. Here lies the cause of that vivid, life like personification to which the prophet subjects the people of Israel, putting words upon their lips expressing a mode of feeling such as, strictly speaking, only an individual can experience. It is his own heart that the prophet has put into the body of Israel. The construction is in the plural, but the spirit is in the singular, and it needs only to be translated back into the singular, to render it a most appropriate speech for every believer in addressing Jehovah: "Come and let us return unto Jehovah; for He hath torn, and He will heal us; He hath smitten and He will bind us up. After two days will He revive us; on the third day He will raise us up, and we shall live before Him. And let us know, let us follow on to know Jehovah: His going forth is sure as the morning; and He will come unto us as the rain, as the latter rain that watereth the earth." And thus the prophet, and through him doubtless others, had the wonderful experience that the God of Israel could give Himself to a single person with the same individual interest and undivided devotion, as if that person were the only one to whom His favor extended. This is necessary to complete the fruition of God. Every child of God, no matter how broad his vision and enlarged his sympathies, is conscious of carrying within himself a private sanctuary, an inner guest-chamber of the heart, where he desires to be at times alone with God and have his Savior to himself. So instinctive and irrepressible is the craving for this, that it may easily give rise to a sort of spiritual jealousy, making it difficult to believe that the God who has given Himself to millions of others should receive us alone into absolute intimacy and show us the secret of His covenant. Does it seem improper to pray, "Come Lord to me alone, and close the door, that I may have Thee to myself for a day and an hour?" Should this feeling come to us and perplex us, the best way to meet it is to consider the existence of the same mystery in the relation of earthly parents to their children. It matters not whether there be one or ten, each child has the full affection of the father's and mother's heart. If we that are creatures can experience the working of this miracle in our finite lives, how much more can the infinite God be present to a countless number of souls and give to each one of them the same ineffable gift? He is God and not man, the Holy One, both in our midst and in our hearts.

Finally, the possession and enjoyment of Jehovah by Israel has according to the prophet a transforming effect. greatest wonder in our fruition of God. This tree, unlike the probation-tree of paradise, has the veritable power of making man like unto God. Those who dwell together in the holy companionship of the covenant grow like unto each other. There is a magic assimilative influence in all the spiritual intimacies of life. But here the mystery is deepest, because it plays between God and man. It works in both directions: as it has caused God's gift of Himself to us to as Here we touch upon the assume even the form of the incarnation, in which He became flesh of our flesh and bone of our bones, so in the opposite direction it makes us partakers of the divine nature, putting upon our souls God's image and superscription. This is not, of course, the fusing of two entities; such a thought lay far from Hosea's mind. It is the interpenetration of the two conscious lives of God and man, each holding the other in the close embrace of a perfect sympathy. The prophet has developed this thought also in connection with the marriage idea. As the wife becomes like unto the husband, and the husband unto the wife, through the daily association of years, so Israel, the wife of Jehovah, is bound to undergo an inner change through which the features of God are slowly but surely wrought out in her character. The beauty of the Lord God is put upon her. This law works with absolute necessity. The prophet traces it even in the shameful pagan cult, which in other respects is the caricature of the true religion of Israel. Those who come to Baal-Peor and consecrate themselves to the shameful thing become abominable like that which they love. The principle laid down applies to all idolatry, open or disguised; whatever man substitutes for the living God as an object of his supreme devotion not only turns into his master, but ends with becoming a superimposed character fashioning him irresistibly into likeness with itself. There is no worshipper but bears the image of his God. The self-sovereignty and independence affected by sin are not allowed to exist. With a sure nemesis religion reclaims its own and in each one of its pseudo-forms thrusts man back into the attitude of worship. Likeness to God, however, is not merely the effect of his giving Himself to us, it is also the condition on which the reality of such divine self-communication is suspended. To have God and to be owned by God in the profound covenant sense would be impossible and result in doing violence to the nature of God and man alike, if the character of man could not be made to fit into the nature and will of God. The basis of all religion is that man must exist in the image of God. Only On This Basis Can The Further Assimilation Proceed. But the prophet has given this thought the warm baptism of affection. A power of conscious love is at work in the process. To bring out his own image in Israel is the delight of Israelis lover and husband. This is the reason why the likeness is represented as beginning with the day of betrothal, and the chief qualities entering into it appear as a bridal gift from God to Israel, God giving her, as it were, of his own attributes: "I will betroth thee unto me in righteousness and in justice, in lovingkindness and in mercies, and thou shalt know Jehovah." That The Gift Is a gift of likeness appears also in this, that it is equivalent to the knowledge of Jehovah. Hence the emphasis thrown on the need of knowledge in Hosea's prophecy. God is declared to have known Israel in the wilderness, in the land of great drought. And of Israel it is required, "Thou shalt know no God but me." In both cases the meaning of the word goes far beyond the intellectual sphere; to know is not a mere act or process of becoming informed, but an act of sympathetic absorption in the other's character. It describes Jehovah's original choice of Israel as a most affectionate determination of what Israel was to be, and the attitude of the people as a passionate searching after the perfections of the divine nature. It is that self-projection of the lover into the beloved which is more than knowledge through the understanding. Hence also the trait of eagerness which the prophet ascribes to it. It is not a state of contentment, but partakes of the extreme restlessness of love in motion: "O' let us know, let us follow on to know Jehovah!" This is to such an extent the heart and soul of the marriage, that the one great adultery consists in this: that Israel does not know, and does not care to know Jehovah. For that is to fail of the End for Which the covenant exists; it makes the marriage idle and fruitless. And finally, my hearers, from this falls some light upon the mystery that a finite creature can receive and possess the infinite God. To speak of giving and possession and enjoyment is after all but speaking in figures. When we try to resolve the figure into the thing itself, the reality grows so great and deep that it transcends our minds, and we must resign ourselves to an experience without understanding. But here is something that we can at least make relatively clear to ourselves: the fruition of God consists in the reception by us of his likeness into ourselves, so that his beauty of character becomes literally our own. So close and so precious an identification no other love can dream of and no other union attain. In it the fruit and the tree become one; we feel and taste that the Lord is for our delight. And When that picture, which Hosea saw as in a glass darkly through the tracings of the imagery of lily and olive-tree and grain and wine, when that picture shall have resolved itself for us into the spiritual realities of the life to come, then also the covenant climax will have been reached, every sacrament shall fall away, and our fruition shall be of God within God; we shall at last be like Him, because we know Him as He is.

II. Hungering and Thirsting After Righteousness

Matthew 5:6
"Blessed are they that hunger and thirst after
righteousness, for they shall he filled"

The Sermon on the Mount is rightly accorded a chief place in the teaching of our Lord. It carries a weight of authority, sets an ethical standard, and reveals heights and depths of the religious life, nowhere surpassed in the Gospels. The Evangelists in recording it seem to have been aware of this. Matthew does not, as on other occasions, introduce the discourse with the conventional phrase "Jesus said," but with the quite solemn statement "And He opened his mouth," thus giving us to understand that the utterance of these words was to Jesus' own mind an act to which He deliberately proceeded. And Luke conveys somewhat of the same impression by the introductory statement, "And He lifted up his eyes on the disciples and said. "Jesus never spoke without a clear sense of the consequence with which his words were fraught. And blessed is the preacher of whom it can be truly said that ministering the Word of God is to him an holy task. But, while the sense of this was always present with our Lord, it was heightened on this occasion. This was the first time that He set Himself to teach His disciples. Here He assumes that peculiar ministry of breaking the bread of life for his own, which He has ever since unceasingly performed through the ages, and even now performs for us, as in these moments we gather round his feet to receive his teaching. In fact it is here for the first time that the term "disciples" occurs in Matthew's Gospel. Hence also the statement that our Lord "sat down," and, having made the disciples draw near, so taught them. The sitting posture, with the hearers standing around, was characteristic of the relation between teacher and pupils, in distinction from the standing position, marking the prophet or gospel-herald.

To note these details of description is not of merely historical interest, but also of practical religious importance, because it may warn us at the outset against a view all too commonly prevailing concerning the purpose of this "Sermon on the Mount. "The sermon is often represented as a succinct summary of Jesus' message. It passes for an epitome of Christianity, the test stone of what is essential to our religion. All that is not here, we are told, can without detriment be neglected. Every later type of Christian life and teaching is to be judged, not by the standard of Scripture as a whole, nor even by the authority of the words of Christ as a whole, but by the content of this one discourse. This deplorable error is due to more than one cause. The beauty and glory truth concentrated here may easily beget a feeling that all else in the New Testament is in comparison of minor value. A second motive coming into play is that many people in the matter of religious belief wholly abandon themselves to their ungoverned tastes and feelings. They scorn every hard and fast rule of faith and practice. Even submission to the indiscriminate teaching of Jesus they find distasteful. At the same time, unwilling to appear entirely emancipated from all historical bonds of faith, they fall back upon some choice portion of the Gospel, preferably the Sermon on the Mount, and cling to it as to the last remaining shreds of the garment of creed, barely sufficient to cover the nakedness of their subjectivity. It is thus that the Sermon on the Mount has become the creed of the creedless. But by far the most influential force driving people to such a view comes from the flattery it supplies to the natural man. It flatters him by taking for granted that he needs no more than the presentation of this high ideal, and that Jesus does him the honor of thinking him capable of realizing it by his own natural goodness. And, last of all, it is not so much what people find in the Sermon on the Mount, it is what they congratulate themselves upon not finding there, that renders them thus enamored of its excellence. It is because they dislike the story of the helplessness of sin, of man's utter condemnation in the sight of God, and the insistence upon the necessity of the cross, it is because of all this that they evince such eagerness to adopt as their exclusive creed a portion of the Gospel from which in their opinion these offensive things are absent. Now all such forget that both Jesus and the Evangelist expressly relate the Sermon on the Mount to the disciples, and consequently place back of what is described in it the process of becoming a disciple, the whole rich relationship of saving approach and responsive faith, of calling and repentance and pardon and acceptance and the following of Jesus, all that makes the men and women of the Gospel such disciples and Jesus such a Lord and Savior as this and other records of his teachings imply. It is therefore folly to insist that no specific doctrine of salvation is here. It Is Present as a living doctrine incarnate in the Person of Jesus. We are apt to forget that in the days of our Lord's flesh there was no need for that explicit teaching about the Christ found in the Epistles of the New Testament. At that time He, the real Christ, walked among

men and exhibited in his intercourse with sinners more
impressively than any abstract doctrine could have done the
principles and the process of salvation. If we have but eyes to
see, we shall find our Savior in the outdoor scenes of the
Gospels no less than within the walls of the school of the
Epistle to the Romans. And we shall find Him too in the
Sermon on the Mount. For this discourse throughout
presupposes that the disciples here instructed became
associated with Jesus as sinners needing salvation, and that
their whole life in continuance is lived on the basis of grace.
At the beginning stand the beatitudes, engraven in golden
script upon its portal, reminding us that we are not received
by Jesus into a school of ethics but into a kingdom of
redemption. It is blessedness that is promised here, and the
word does not so much signify a state of mind, as that great
realm of consummation and satisfaction, which renders
man's existence, once he has entered into it, serene and
secure forevermore. And again, foremost among the
beatitudes stand those that emphasize the emptiness, the
absolute dependence of man upon divine grace. As at the
dawn of the gospel Mary sang: "He has put down princes
from their thrones, and has exalted them of low degree; the
hungry He has filled with good things and the rich He has
sent empty away, "so here those pronounced blessed are the
poor in spirit, the mourners, the meek, and they that hunger
and thirst after righteousness. It is in no wise to the self-
satisfied mind that the Lord addresses Himself; his call is not
a call to exertion, not even to exertion in holiness; it were
too little to say that it is an invitation to receive; it goes

farther than that; it amounts to the declaration that the consciousness of having nothing, absolutely nothing, is the certain pledge of untold enrichment. So much is salvation a matter of giving on God's part that it's best subjects are those in whom his grace of giving can have its perfect work. The poor in spirit, those that mourn, the meek and the hungry, these are made to pass before our eyes as so many typical forms of its embodiment. And because this is so, they are here also introduced as having the promise of the infinite. To be a child of God and a disciple of Jesus means to hold in one's hand the treasures of eternity. Look for a moment at the second clauses of these beatitudes. Some of the things spoken of may, in a relative sense, be obtained in the present life. Comfort and mercy and the vision of God and sonship are bestowed during our pilgrimage on earth. As a matter of fact, however, these things are here held in prospect not in relative but in absolute measure. In the consummate life only can it become true that the meek inherit the earth, that the eyes of the pure behold the beatific vision of God, that the hungry and thirsty are satisfied with righteousness. This absolute character of the promise writes the principle of redemption large on the face of the Sermon on the Mount. To join together after this manner creature-emptiness and the riches of divine benediction is the prerogative of God the Savior. So long as this voice of the beatitudes is distinctly heard, it will not be possible to find any other religion here than the religion of salvation through the grace of God in Christ.

But is it not true, you are perhaps inclined to ask, that at least from the words of our text the opposite view receives a measure of support? "Righteousness"—in this word certainly the stress seems to be laid on ethical conduct without any particular admixture of the redemptive element. Men are willing to admit that, so far as the specifically religious qualities are concerned, our attitude must be a receptive one, leaving all the energizing to God. When, however, the sphere of the moral life is reached, the principle seems no longer to apply, this being the field of cooperation between the divine and the human. That people are rash to draw such a conclusion is partly due to the modish social coloring which the term "righteousness" receives at the present day. But we may not determine its meaning for our text in the light of this modern association. The important question to answer is what meaning the word carried to the mind of Jesus. As soon as this is done, we shall soon discover that no greater mistake could be made from Jesus' point of view than to assume that in the matter of righteousness the divine is less and the human more than in other relations. It would be crude, to be sure, straightway to inject into our text the doctrine of Paul according to which righteousness is something wrought out in Christ and transferred to us by imputation. And yet, it would be a far more serious mistake to suppose that our Lord's idea of righteousness and that of Paul differed in principle and did not grow from the same root. There need be no difficulty in showing that Jesus, and in fact all preceding revelation, carefully laid the basis for this crowning structure of

Apostolic revelation. In order to do this let us note in the first place that righteousness is in Scripture an idea saturated with the thought of God. Throughout the Old Testament this is so. It is a commonplace of its teaching, especially in the prophets, that there can be no true obedience of heart and life without the constant presence to the mind of man of the thought of Jehovah. Not only is ethics without religion a fragmentary thing; even more important is the principle that in such a case it lacks the true quality of right, the inner essence of what renders it conformable to its very idea. Righteousness is the opposite of sin, and as the reference to God is inseparable from the conception of sin, so the reference to God is in precisely the same manner inherent in the idea of righteousness. To put it very plainly: If there were no God to see and judge and punish, one might perhaps still continue to speak of good and evil, meaning thereby what is beneficial or injurious, subject to the approval or disapproval of men, but it would be meaningless to speak of sin on such a supposition. And so, by equal reasoning, while what is commonly called good might without the existence of God be conceivable in the world, yet it could not properly bear the name of righteousness, for the simple reason that, in order to deserve this name, according to the Biblical way of thinking, it needs first to be placed in the light of the divine nature, the divine will, the divine judgment. At the very birth of the people of God this principle was embedded deep in their life, when God said to Abraham: "I am El-Shaddai, walk thou before me, then shalt thou be blameless." To walk before God means so to walk as

to have the thought of God's presence and supervision
constantly in mind, and to shape one's conduct accordingly.
Our Lord's whole teaching on the subject of righteousness is
but one emphatic reaffirmation and further development of
the same principle. Although the religious atmosphere in his
day was surcharged with the notions of law-keeping and
merit and retribution, there was lacking the vivid
consciousness of God as a perpetual witness and interested
participant in every moral transaction. The automaton of the
law had taken the place of the living God. Well might our
Lord quote the words of the prophet Isaiah "This people
honoreth me with their lips, but their heart is far from me."
Alas, this fault with which Jesus had to contend is not so
exclusively peculiar to the spirit of that age as we might
perhaps be inclined to assume. A Jew lives in you and me
and in every human heart by nature. If we ever were
tempted to think ourselves able to fulfill the law of God, was
it not perhaps for this reason—that the sense of God's
absolute claim upon us and knowledge of us had become
dim to our conscience? Since, then, this fault reappears in
every sinner, the Preacher of the Mount repeats his sermon
in the ears of each generation. He stands to plead the right of
God, no matter what substitutes for Him we may have put
up in our lives, nay not even though it were, as in the case of
Judaism, a counterfeit of God's own law. And, great
physician that He is. He directs his probe straight to the root
of the disease. Christ drives us back into the inner chambers
of our consciousness, where God and we are alone, and
good and evil assume a proportion and significance never

dreamt of before. The law in the hands of Jesus becomes alive with God's own personality. Majestic and authoritative. He is present in every commandment, so absolute in his demands, so observant of our conduct, so intent upon the outcome, that the thought of giving to Him less than heart and soul and mind and strength in the product of our moral life ceases to be tolerable to ourselves. Much has been preached and written about the internal character of the law observance which the Sermon on the Mount requires. Truly, it does teach with powerful emphasis that the righteousness is in the intent and disposition, not first in the outward act, just as the sin is not committed first when the hand reaches out to strike, but when anger surges up in the heart. But we do not, I am afraid, realize with sufficient clearness what is the ultimate reason for this internalizing emphasis. Why are evil and good with such insistency pushed back into the region of the heart? The reason is none other than that in the heart man confronts God. In the recesses of the inner man, where deep calls unto deep, where the Lawgiver and the creature are face to face, there and there alone the issue of righteousness and o sin can be decided. Nor does this merely mean that the conscience is brought under the direct gaze and control of the will of God. It is the divine nature lying back of the divine will in the light of which the creature is led to place itself. The inner man enters, if we may so speak, into the inner forum of the Most High. There God, besides requiring obedience to his will, is heard to ask conformity to his moral nature. The law is perceived to coincide with what He is. The majesty, the inevitableness, the self-evidencing and self-enforcing power of the eternal are put into it. To fulfill the law becomes but another form of the imperative, to be like unto God. It is God's inalienable right as God to impress his character upon us, to make and keep us reflectors of his infinite glory. But in a state of sin this can only intensify a thousand times the consciousness of man's utter inability even to begin to realize what nevertheless is the very core of his end in life, the sole ultimate reason for his existence. Thus apprehended the range and scope of the moral circle drawn around our being become enormous, so much so indeed that they would almost seem to exceed the possibilities of frail human nature. So long as man's moral life is not illumined by this central glory of the nature of God, it may remain possible for the illusion to spring up that the sinner can at least aspire towards fulfilment of the law. He then imagines that the command is relaxed and lowered to the limitations of his abnormal state. The limitless perspective, all that makes for the eternal seriousness and solemnity of the values of righteousness and sin, are forgotten. "To be righteous" acquire the restricted meaning of being law like, instead of God-like. Sin also loses its absolute character of disharmony with the divine nature. It appears a mere shortness in one's account, easily rectifiable by future extra payments. To all this delusion Jesus puts an end by the simple word "Ye shall be perfect as your Father in heaven is perfect," and: "Thus shall ye pray: Thy will be done, as in heaven so on earth." And, still further, the purpose of this demand of God-likeness is not to be primarily sought in the desirability for man of patterning himself after the highest example; it has its deeper ground in the right of God to possess and use us as instruments for the revelation of his supreme glory. If God desires to mirror Himself in us, can it behoove man to offer Him less than a perfect reflection? Shall we say, that He must overlook the little blemishes, the minor sins, the mixed aspirations, the half-hearted efforts, must take the will for the deed, and an imperfect will at that? Or shall we confess with the speaker in Job that the heavens are not clean in his sight? Once this point of view is adopted, our whole estimate of sin and righteousness undergoes a radical change. We then begin to measure and appraise them in their bearing on God and their value for Him. Obedience becomes sacrifice; the light that is in us no longer shines for our own delectation, but in order that through the perception of our good works by men glory may come to our Father in heaven. Here lies also the reason why, notwithstanding all the emphasis placed on the secretness and inwardness of righteousness, our Lord none the less insists upon the necessity of works as essential to the issue of the moral process. Because it does not exist for itself, therefore the right must leap to the light of day. Jesus, no more than Paul, would have assented to the view that in sanctification the good will or intention is the sole thing required. The tree of righteousness is planted in us by God for his own sake, and consequently He delights in its blossoms and desires to eat of its fruit.

We have now explored a little of the length and breadth and height and depth of what the Sermon on the Mount proclaims as the whole duty of man. The task of fulfilling this is so stupendous that a sinless being might almost contemplate it with misgiving. Where, then, shall the ungodly and sinner appear? Can our Lord have meant that it is even remotely possible for the disciple by his own strength to attain unto this? Our text implies the very opposite. No, not the possession of such a righteousness is characteristic of the members of the kingdom, but that they hunger and thirst after it. Notice sharply the implications of the striking figure employed. It implies, of course, in the first place that the disciple has not in himself, and is conscious of not having, the thing described. That, however, is only the negative side; to the absence there corresponds the desire for its presence. And a very specific kind of desire is referred to. Its strength is emphasized, and that not merely in general, but in the very particular sense of its being an elemental desire, a life-craving, in which the deepest instincts of the disciple assert themselves. To hunger and thirst after a thing means the recognition that without that thing there can be no life. It involves that in this one desire and its satisfaction the whole meaning of life is centered, that the whole energy of life is directed towards it, that the goal of life is identified with it. To the sense of this fundamental spiritual craving all other things are obliterated. As to the hungry and thirsty gold and silver become worthless, so to the disciple in whom this desire has awakened, the wealth of the universe, where he offered it, would have no attraction. And let us remember that this intensified desire has for its object the righteousness of God as previously described. What renders this thing desirable is the vision of it as associated with God.

In its ultimate analysis it is the passion for God Himself. Here is the cry of the Psalmist: "Whom have I in heaven but Thee, and there is none upon earth that I desire besides Thee, "translated into terms of ethics. Still further, the form of hunger and thirst which the desire assumes presupposes the clearest conceivable perception of the nature of its object. As there is no more vivid picture of the nourishing and refreshing power of food and drink than that which stands before the imagination of a hungry and thirsty person, so there is no truer, no more adequate reproduction of God's own idea of righteousness than that which exists in the mind that hungers and thirsts after the manner here portrayed. Herein lies one of the chief glories of the work of redemption, that it produces in the heart and mind of the sinner such a profound, ineffaceable impression of the realities in God. Nothing will lay so bare the foundations of our relationship to Him as the experience of salvation. The thing spoken of in the text appears nowhere else in such an intense form as it does through its connection with sin. The beginning of hungering and thirsting after righteousness lies in the birth of conviction of sin. In fact the presence of this element in it is what distinguishes true, deep repentance from every kind of superficial regret for the secondary consequences of sin. True repentance strips sin of all that is accidental. It resembles an inner chamber where no one and nothing else is admitted except God and the sinner and his sin. Into that chamber all the great penitents like David and Paul and Augustine and Luther have entered, and each one in the bitter anguish of his soul has borrowed the words of the Psalmist: "Against Thee, Thee only have I sinned, and done this evil in thy sight, that Thou mightest be justified when Thou speakest, and be clear when Thou judgest." A repentant sinner acquits God and condemns himself. And for the very reason that his consciousness of sin is God-centered, he is also alive to its inward seriousness. He learns to trace it in the recesses and abysses of his inmost life, where even the eye of self-scrutiny would otherwise scarcely penetrate, but in which the eyes of God are at home, where all our iniquities stand naked before Him and our secret sins in the light of his countenance. If it is characteristic of sin to excuse itself, it is no less characteristic of repentance to scorn all subterfuge and to judge of itself, as it were, with the very veracity of God. Herein indeed is shown the first grace of God to an awakened sinner that He lets in upon the soul this cleansing flood of moral truth. It is a painful experience, but even through the pain the penitent feels that his relation towards God has been in principle rectified, that the sorrow of repentance is a sorrow after God Himself. Without that much of faith there is no repentance, by that much of faith gracious repentance differs from the remorse of the hopelessly lost. And from such saving penitence there is but one more step to the recognition that the claims of the divine righteousness in their widest extent must be satisfied. To a mind thus disposed the thought of atonement is no longer an offense or foolishness, but something commending itself by its inherent justice. The doctrine of satisfaction ages before it was elaborated by religious thinkers had vindicated itself, as it still continues to do, to thousands of hearts in the bitter theology of repentance. The fact of sin, while as such irrevocably accomplished, yet so far as the guilt is concerned must be undone, if God is to remain the God of sinners. Here the truth taught by-Jesus leads directly to Paul's doctrine of atonement and justification. To the heart that has had the Sermon on the Mount interpreted to itself by the Holy Spirit there is no other solution and refuge than the cross underneath which Paul found shelter. To such as hunger and thirst after righteousness the flesh of the Son of Man is meat and his blood is drink, indeed.

But the principle expressed in our text reaches still farther out. The hungering and thirsting most assuredly also include a desire to exhibit the righteousness of discipleship in a sanctified life. And this Christian pursuit of holiness likewise is centered in God. It is not as if in justification the divine grace, and in sanctification human endeavor, were the sole factor to be reckoned with. Much rather in sanctification itself the old alternative again presents itself, whether in all its parts, in the acting upon by God and in the being moved to responsive action of the believer, the divine glory or human merit shall be the principal concern. There is a striving after moral excellence in which the selfish sinful nature most vigorously reasserts itself, involving merely a transition from the gross and carnal to the more refined and elusive type of sin. The true disciple does not seek to be made better for his own glory but in the interest and for the glory of God. He feels with Paul that he must apprehend, because he was apprehended for that very purpose. The image of God restored in the soul cannot help turning back towards its original. The new man is created after God in righteousness and holiness of truth. The believer, therefore, sanctifies himself, that God's purpose may not be frustrated in him, but find glorious fruition. Only he does so in constant reliance on divine grace. It were a mistake to confine the province of faith to justification. All progress in holiness depends on it. It is the element, the atmosphere in which the Christian lives, that which imparts to his works their sacrificial character and makes them pleasing to God. And, because, thanks to God, it is deeper in him than his deepest sin, even when he fails and falls, he does not despair, nor is utterly forsaken. God's witness remains in him; he can say with Peter: "Lord, Thou knowest all things. Thou knowest that I love Thee!"

Finally, the Lord here assures the hungry and thirsty ones, that they shall be satisfied. Every instinctive desire, when normal, carries in itself the knowledge that there is that which can satisfy it. The great gifts of God and the great desires of life have been created for each other, and call for each other. If this be true in the natural world, it is equally true in the spiritual world, in the sphere of redemption. The craving described in our text is a prophecy; it tells of a law in the kingdom of God, a sure creative appointment, out of which, twin children of the divine grace, the hunger after righteousness and the righteousness itself are born. It is God, and God alone, who can produce in the deepest heart of man a thing so instinctive as what is here spoken of. No sinner can give this to himself. If we feel it at all, to however slight a degree, it is from no other cause than that the love of God has found us, and the breath of the Spirit Creator has blown upon us, quickening us into newness of life. If this were a de-sire artificially awakened or stimulated by man, there could be no assurance of either the existence or the satisfying character of its object. Even in the case of our noblest and most elevating desires after the creature, we too often make sad experience of the failure of our ideals to meet the expectation. There a son is that in our dreams we ourselves are the creators of the excellence we crave, and because we cannot also create the satisfaction, we hunger in vain. But it is different here. He that gave the thirst likewise provides the water, and the one exactly meets the other. It is not the will of our Heavenly Father that any longing in our hearts, prompted by Himself, and therefore sincerely seeking Him, shall perish unsatisfied. A satisfying righteousness therefore must be provided for the people of God. And it must be provided outside of us. To eat means to be nourished from without. Since the sinner is devoid of all righteousness, it is self-evident, that the source of his supply must be sought beyond the confines of his own evil and empty nature. For it to be otherwise would mean that hunger could be stilled with hunger. Our Lord's meaning obviously is that the coming order of things, the new kingdom of God, brings with itself, chief of all blessings, a perfect righteousness, as truly and absolutely the gift of God to man as is the entire kingdom. What is true of the kingdom, that no human merit can deserve, no human effort call it into being, applies with equal force to the righteousness that forms its center. It is God's creation, not man's. The prophet recognized it as such when, despairing of sinful Israel, he promised that in the future, in the new covenant, God would remember the sin no more, and would write his law upon the tablets of the heart. Our Lord here simply declares that what prophets and psalmists saw from afar is on the point of becoming real. The acceptable year of Jehovah is about to begin. His Beatitudes are the evangel, giving answer across the ages to the prophecies of old. It means that with comfort and riches and mercy and sonship and the vision of God, righteousness will be given in abundance to a destitute people. True, Jesus does not enter here upon any description of the method by which this is to be accomplished. As little as He specifies what will bring comfort in the place of mourning, does He tell how righteousness will banish sin. But does not the very fact of his foregoing to tell this afford a presumption that He is conscious of carrying the source and substance of all these things in his own Person? The same Jesus who immediately afterwards in interpreting the law puts side by side with the commandment of God his sovereign, "I say unto you," the same Jesus here takes into his hands all the riches of prophecy, as only the God of prophecy can take them, and disposes of them as his own sovereign gift: "Theirs is the kingdom," and "They shall be filled." What gives Him the right to speak thus, not merely in the sphere of power, but also in the sphere of righteousness? As God He could change sickness into health, and mourning into joy, but even as God He cannot change sin and guilt into righteousness by a mere fiat of his will. When, nevertheless, He here declares that

this will be done, the reason is that in his own life, his life of
a servant, this greatest of all tasks is being accomplished. In
one sense the Sermon on the Mount was a sermon preached
out of his own personal experience. The righteousness He
described was not a distant ideal, it was an incarnate reality
in Himself. He alone of all mankind fulfilled the law in its
deepest purport and widest extent. His keeping of it
proceeded from that sanctuary of his inner life where He and
the Father always beheld each other's face. He made it his
meat and drink to do the will of God. His human nature was
an altar from which the incense of perfect consecration rose
ceaselessly day and night. He submitted to the cross and
endured the shame, not merely on our behalf, but first of all
in order that not one jot or one tittle of the divine justice
should fall to the ground. He not only hungered and thirsted
but was satisfied with the travail of his soul. And now you
and I can come and take of the bread and water of life freely.
Through justification we are even in this life filled with the
fulness of his merit, and appear to God as spotless and
blameless as though sin had never touched us. Through
sanctification his holy character is impressed upon our souls,
so that, notwithstanding our imperfections, God takes a true
delight in us, seeing that the inner man is changed from day
to day after the likeness of Christ. And the full meaning of
our Lord's promise we shall know in the last day, when He
shall satisfy Himself in us by presenting us to God perfect in
body, soul and Spirit. Then shall come to pass the word that
is written "They shall hunger no more, neither thirst

anymore." For we shall behold God's face in righteousness
and be satisfied, when we awake, with his image.

57

III. Seeking and Saving the Lost

Luke 19:10:

"For the Son of Man came to seek and to save that
which was lost."

The words of our text are Jesus' own commentary on the event described in the preceding verses. His meeting with Zacchaeus and, as a result of this, the publican's salvation, were in the last analysis due to the fact, that the Son of Man came to seek and to save that which was lost. And in the light of this interpretation the event itself in turn becomes a commentary upon the Savior's ministry in the largest sense, both upon that which He served while on earth and upon that which He now fulfills, walking through the lands and the ages, as He once walked through the fields and cities of Palestine. Neither this nor any other occurrence in the Gospel-history was a casual thing. It is true, these days of our Lord's flesh which He lived among his countrymen, acting and acted upon, were a real concrete piece of life interwoven with the life of Israel. They belong to that age and generation as truly as any section of human history can be said to belong to the times in which it happened. But it is also true that this is not common history, but sacred, redemptive history, which means that there runs through it, from beginning to end, a special design, ordering its course, shaping its frame, and fixing its issues, so as to make of it a proper stage for the enactment of the great mystery of redemption, whose spectators and participants were not merely the Jews of that age but the inhabitants of all subsequent ages. Nothing is casual here; every moment, every circumstance, every person that our Lord touched became fraught by that touch with a profound actuality and an eternal significance. How marvelously adapted was the setting of these scenes to serve their unique purpose! What sharp contrasts of human state and condition were here brought together! What pronounced types of sin, exhibiting in their development the root principles of all evil, appear side by side! The Pharisee and the Publican come together to the temple of God! Truly, in this world of the Jewish land a microcosmic picture was presented of the realms of sin and suffering and sorrow and death. And because this is so, you and I can come to the story of two thousand years ago and find a present salvation there, an ever open door to the house of peace and hope. These are not strange, outlandish scenes and surroundings we are invited to; it is the familiar ground of sin and salvation; those who people it are flesh of our flesh and bone of our bone, and the Savior, who comes to meet them, in their persons meets us and transacts his business with us individually about matters of eternal importance.

For a few moments with the statement of our text in mind let us look at what passed between Zacchaeus and the Savior. The time is that of Jesus' last journey to Jerusalem shortly before the great Passover in which all things were to be fulfilled. These were the last hours of the day during which it is possible to work; closer and closer drew near for Him that night of suffering and death in which it is not given to any man to work. Could one have wondered, if in this critical hour our Lord's thoughts had been wholly turned forward and inward, if, oblivious to his surroundings, He had been intent upon the tremendous experience of his passion with which He was now almost face to face? We do find Him faithful and busy in the outward duty until the last moment. As He loved his own until the end, so it may be said that He sought his own until the darkness of death closed in upon Him. But a moment ago He had helped the blind beggar at the entrance to Jericho, and, scarcely within the city, a publican becomes the object of his quest. Notice how vividly the sense of a specific duty, here and now to be performed, is present to the Savior's mind, for He announces to Zacchaeus: "Today I must abide at thine house." His times and ways and works were not his own—but the Father's who had sent Him. But let us further notice the precise expression that principle receives in the statement: "The Son of Man came to seek and to save that which was lost." There is no need of asking for the moment, whence He came; the fact of his coming in itself sufficiently claims our attention. For this "coming" means his coming into the world it covers his entire earthly life; He was born for this purpose, and this purpose only, to seek and save the lost. Never in all human history was there such an absolute concentration of life upon a single specific task as that which our Lord here affirms of Himself. Every man comes into the world to work out a design of God in his existence. But in the case of each one of us this design embraces a number of various ends, all of which we legitimately pursue, and in all of which we serve the will of God. Our Lord's life was a human life which derived its meaning from beginning to end from his vocation as a Savior; in seeking and saving its significance exhausted itself. To that even the most sacred and private concerns of his soul with God, his prayer, his trust, all his intercourse with the Father, were wholly

subservient. The personal was swallowed up in the one great
devotion to the work of God. Into this the full stream of his
strength flowed, from this its hidden sources were
nourished: He made it his meat and his drink to do the will
of his Father in heaven. He lived for this will and He lived on
it. Thus only can we explain to ourselves the sensitiveness of
our Lord, where his right to prosecute this task was called
into question, for then He felt Himself assailed in the center
and sanctuary of his being. Hence on this very occasion,
when after his entrance of the house of Zacchaeus the people
murmured, saying, "He is gone in to lodge with a man that
is a sinner," our Lord did not content Himself with pointing
out the propriety and beneficence of the act, but vindicated
his conduct by an appeal to the supreme law of life under
which He stood and from which He could not free Himself
without ceasing to be what He was. With what sublime
simplicity He takes for granted, that his entering into a
house could be for no other purpose than to introduce
salvation there! Of course, there is in this something unique,
incapable of reproduction in precisely that sense by even the
most consecrated servant of God. He was made incarnate
for the work of salvation, and we are dedicated to our
ministry on the basis of a natural life we already possess.
Paul perhaps in this respect approached nearest to the
example of the Lord, having been separated from his
mother's womb for the Apostleship. In his words, "Woe is
me, if I preach not the Gospel" we imagine to hear an echo
of our text and other similar declarations of our Lord. But
surely, though with an almost equal distance between, we

likewise ought to possess some reproduction of this mind of Christ within us. Pitiable indeed is the plight of the steward of Christ, who can not say from a conviction as profound as the roots of his spiritual life itself, that he came into the kingdom for the very purpose of seeking and of saving that which was lost.

The Lord's statement, however, obtains a still richer and more forceful meaning by our enquiring whence and out of what state He came to enter upon this life task. It may be in a certain sense true that in the Synoptical Gospels there is not that emphatic expression of his eternal pre-existence in the world of heaven, not that sublime consciousness of transcending the sphere of time, as are met within the discourses recorded by John. But, surely, if we will only come to them with believing minds, we shall not fail to find even in these simpler narratives indications of the great mystery of godliness sufficiently clear to satisfy us, when in the helplessness of our sins we cry out for a divine, an eternal Savior. Such a message our text brings us, when it declares that "the Son of Man came to seek and to save that which was lost." The word "came" is in itself suggestive of a previous sphere and state which He exchanged for our world, a sphere and state wherein no seeking nor saving was required, because there all live secure and blessed in God. But much more suggestive is this word when coupled with the name "Son of Man." It is not accidental that our Lord makes use of this self-designation in a connection like this. Elsewhere also we read that "The Son of Man came not to be ministered unto but to minister and to give his life a ransom." And in a number of other passages the title is associated with his abode in the world of heaven, whence He descended to these lower regions of ours. In the prophecy of Daniel, where first the phrase "Son of Man" is used to describe the Messiah, twice a "coming" is affirmed of the Person so designated: "There came with the clouds of heaven One like unto a son of man, and He came even to the Ancient of Days." Now, while our Lord often identifies the "coming" thus described with his return to judgment, yet He likewise once and again retrospectively associates it with his first advent, when He came out of the glory He had with the Father before the world was. Being told, therefore, that it was the "Son of Man," who came to seek and to save, our first thought surely should be of that unspeakable grace of our Lord, who, being rich as God alone can be rich, yet for our sake became poor as sinful man only can be poor, that by his poverty we might be made rich. The depth to which this seeking and saving brings Him down should be measured by the distance there is between the highest in God and the lowest in man. To lodge with publicans and sinners might be condescension for a high-placed personage what language will express its meaning in the case of the infinite God? The "Son of Man," who unites in Himself all that Deity and humanity together can lend of glory to the Messianic state, He it is who came to seek and to save the lost. It was such a glorious life that was wholly given up to its very last thought, poured out to the very last residue of its strength, and that for the task of helping us, the lowest of us, who would have turned away from one another, because the sinful felt it a degradation to stoop to such as were a degree more sinful than they acknowledged themselves to be. When we combine this consciousness of ineffable glory sacrificed with the consciousness of absolute surrender to the service of the most despised, then, and only then, do we begin to understand somewhat of the indignation with which Jesus repudiated the charge, brought by sinful men, that it was unworthy of Him to associate with publicans and sinners. With superhuman dignity the one word "Son of Man" silences that voice of murmuring in the streets of Jericho, and every echo, we may add, of that same voice from any quarter, or any age, when it presumes to criticize the Gospel of Christ on the ground that it speaks in accents of the sovereign grace of God.

But the fact that He came as the "Son of Man" is important for our Lord's seeking and saving of the lost in still another respect. By reason of it He retains even on earth the exercise of that divine knowledge and power which such a task calls into requisition. Love is farsighted and wields great influence, but love alone, even divine love alone, would not be sufficient to find and save the sinner. Seeking and saving are acts in which God puts forth his omniscience and omnipotence, as the searcher of hearts and the Lord of spirits. To these divine prerogatives the "Son of Man" lays claim in the pursuit of his task. He brings to it all the qualifications which its character as a strictly divine work requires. When making to Nathanael the marvelous disclosure of his supernatural knowledge, He declares, "Ye shall see this heaven opened and the Angels of God ascending and descending upon the Son of Man." It is in the "Son of Man" that the mystic ladder, which Jacob saw at Bethel, has been truly set up, so that God visits man, and man is made aware of the saving presence of God. In healing the sick of the palsy He demonstrated the authority of the "Son of Man" to forgive sins on earth by bidding him arise, take up his bed and go to his house. Here the very point in question was, whether during his sojourn on earth such power belonged to the "Son of Man." That He possessed it in his heavenly state even the Scribes would scarcely have doubted; what they disputed was that any person on earth should pretend to share this right with God. But Jesus claims, and by the miracle proves his claim, that He is on earth invested with the power of saying to a guilty soul, "Thy sins are forgiven thee," and to say it so that the conscience, which obeys no other voice than the voice of God Himself, will acknowledge Him as its Sovereign and be silent at his behest. But what need to look for illustrations elsewhere, when the connection of our text itself gives the most striking example of how our Lord places these divine attributes in the service of his seeking and saving love? When Jesus came to the spot where Zacchaeus had stationed himself for observation, it was surely not by accident that his eye discovered the publican amidst the branches of the tree. His looking up precisely at that point may convince us that He acted deliberately; it was a step in that process of seeking for which He had come. He calls the publican by name, though to all appearance the two had never met before. Yea before that spot on the roadside was reached. He had not only discovered his person, but had read with omniscience the inner-most thoughts of his heart. He who could say, "Before Philip called thee, when thou wast under the fig tree, I saw thee," He had likewise seen Zacchaeus in advance of the latter's seeing Him. Here is a look from which no man can hide himself, the same that saw our first parents behind the branches of the fateful trees, and has since that hour, wherever sinners seek to conceal themselves, penetrated into the recesses of their guilt and shame, called them up from their depths of despair and brought them down from their heights of pride, a look from the eyes of the Lord which are in all places and see the small no less than the great. More than this, we need not hesitate to affirm that the publican, though unaware of the fact, was there at his station by the appointment of Jesus. In all probability Zacchaeus in his desire to see Jesus, who He was, was not so exclusively actuated by curiosity as is usually assumed. But suppose it to have been curiosity and nothing more, even that was in no wise exempt from the Lord's control. Open to Him are a thousand ways to bring you and me to the very place and point where He desires to meet us. How many of us would have been saved, if the Lord had waited till we sought Him out? Thanks be to God, He is a Savior who seeks the lost, who with eyes supernaturally farsighted discerns us a long way off, and draws our interest to Himself by the sweet constraint of his grace, till we are face to face with Him and our soul is saved. As once, in the incarnation, He came down from heaven to seek mankind, so He still comes down silently from heaven in the case of each sinner, and pursues his search for that individual soul following it through all the mazes of its waywardness and the devious paths of its folly, sometimes unto the very brink of destruction, till at last his grace overtakes it and says, "I must lodge at thy house." For, besides the divine omniscience here manifested, we are made witnesses of the Lord's sovereign and almighty power. Having found Zacchaeus Headdresses to him that call, which makes the lame to leap, the blind to see, the deaf to hear, nay the dead to arise, a call like the voice of God at the first creation, "Let there be light, and there was light": "Zacchaeus, make haste and come down, for today I must abide at thine house." Note the instantaneous effect. Behold here Zacchaeus, who perhaps never before had encountered the Savior, who would have hardly ventured to approach Jesus, behold him at a single word trans-formed into a disciple of the Lord. He knows the voice of the Shepherd immediately, makes haste to come down and receives him with joy. This is that wonderful effectual calling by name, which takes place wherever a sinner is saved, and which, while it may not always take place with such suddenness and under such striking circumstances as happened here, yet is in substance everywhere equally supernatural and immediate. The use of the divine word, not only does not detract from its immediacy, but serves the very purpose of expressing the fact that nothing but the omnipotent volition of God is at work in it. For it is characteristic of God, and of God alone, thus to produce effects by a mere word. He gives life to the dead and calls the things that are not, as though they were. Thus Lazarus was summoned from the grave, and thus

Zacchaeus was brought into the Shepherd's fold. Of course, there is no cause for denying that as the result of, and simultaneously with, this call, many thoughts and convictions may be released and spring into action that were previously latent. Images may have floated before Zacchaeus' mind picturing Jesus in his ways and works. The Gospel summons may have come to him through rumor or report of the Savior's life, for even in regard to these outward instrumentalities for conveying the knowledge of Christ it is sometimes true which is written elsewhere concerning the inward birth itself, "The wind bloweth where it listeth, and thou hearest the voice thereof, but knowest not whence it cometh, and whither it goeth." The Spirit of God which makes all things new, can so baptize an ancient fragment of truth, a dimly remembered shadow of knowledge, as to give it in our apperception all the radiant newness of a flash of light fresh from the womb of revelation. But, while all these old elements of consciousness may work, as out of the past, they are in no case the actual producers of the new creature. On the contrary it is only through the immediate impartation of the higher life that they can be roused from their dormant state to the active vitality of a heartfelt experience. Whatever antecedently dwells in our souls of religious knowledge, of reasonable persuasion of the truth, of recognition of God's claim upon us, of stirrings of conscience—it all needs to be regenerated and quickened by the touch of Christ, before it can blossom into saving faith. We speak of our saving men, but this, while conveying a legitimate idea, is a metaphor. At bottom it signifies no more than that through the means of grace we arrange and prepare the situation in which it pleases God to perform the unique saving act. It is ours to let in the light and lay ready the garments which afterwards Lazarus will need, but we cannot wake the sleeper under the stone. Let us rejoice that this is so. Precisely that at the center there lies something that we cannot do constitutes the glory of our message. If the gospel-dispensation were a matter of mere intellectual enlightenment and moral suasion, such as fall within the limits of human power to produce, then indeed it might be urged, that what is reserved for the divine action is subtracted from the scope of human opportunity, the intrusion of God, as it were, diminishing our glory. But on such a view of the gospel ministry its distinction is reduced to a level, where it matters little, whether the minister accomplishes more or less of it. If, on the other hand, the gospel service is incorporated in a creative movement of supernatural character, involving at its core what lies absolutely beyond human power, then to feel this inevitable limitation as a drawback would evince a strange blindness to the most glorious aspect of the preacher's office. To move on the outermost fringe of a process of that kind, to have even the slightest connection with it, confers an unspeakable distinction, because it associates one with what is specifically divine. How much greater still is the grace, if we are permitted not a minimum but the highest conceivable degree of proximity to the wonder world of God! Is not the underlying cause of the failure to perceive this, that we too much individualize and isolate ourselves, instead of feeling

strongly our organic appurtenance to the mighty, super
naturalizing movement introduced by God into this world?
If we could only more adequately realize the irresistible
omnipotence of its momentum and the robe of splendor it
casts around the smallest of its servants, we would exult
with Paul and give thanks to God "who always leadeth us in
triumph in Christ."

But let us return to Zacchaeus and note how our Lord
further illustrates the nature of the saving act for which as
"Son of Man" he claims to possess the full qualifications. It is
an act of seeking and saving the "lost." What it implies can
be ascertained from the state affirmed of its objects. There is
a sure correlation between these two, and, if at any time we
are apt to lose the proper perspective in regard to either of
them, we should immediately rectify our view by reflecting
upon the inherent significance of the other term. The "lost"
are such as require a "Seeker" and "Savior"; when tempted
to dilute or tone down the meaning of this word, it should
suffice to remember, that in the same proportion as this is
done we also detract from the Savior-title of our Lord a
substantial part of its significance. And conversely, if we
allow ourselves to lose sight of even the smallest part of
what the words "to save" and "Savior" connote, it
necessarily modifies the sound which the word "lost" carries
to our ear. There is no escape from this; it is the inherent
logic of the structure of the Gospel. To refuse to be bound
by it puts one beyond the pale of consistent Christianity. It
will therefore well repay us to scan most closely the exact
correspondence of these two ideas in our text. There is

perhaps no passage that enables us to do so to the same degree of definiteness and clearness as this saying of our Lord's. The reason is that here He has, in response to the peculiar situation of Zacchaeus, taken pains to resolve the Savior function in its two component parts, so as to give us a double light for the purpose. The "Son of Man" came not merely to seek, but "to seek and to save. "Nor is this in the nature of a mere addition of a second thing to a first: these two likewise mutually illumine each other; the seeking determines the saving, and the saving in turn the seeking, and both as thus joined together receive their interwoven significance from the "being lost." Now it is not difficult to ascertain what the word "lost" expresses in the vocabulary of Jesus. "To be lost" in its simple, primary sense, which it scarcely needs knowledge of the original to understand, is "to be missing," to have passed out of the active possession and use of one's owner. The word, of course, in order to be intelligible, requires the supplementary thought of a definite possessor. It is not the vague general notion of forsakenness and misery Jesus has in mind when using it, but very particularly the fact of the sinner's being missing to God, that is missing to the normal relations man sustains to God. Because these relations to God constitute in our Lord's opinion the fundamental thing in human life, the state of "being lost" acquires that sad connotation of total derangement and dissolution of all the factors and forces of spiritual existence; the word has about it the solemn, ominous sound of darkness and chaos. The light and health of life, which are religion, have departed with the departure from Him who is the one source of both. The lost sinner is swung out of the orbit appointed for him by the central position of God, deprived of all the attractions of fellowship and trust and obedience and blessedness that were his birthright ever since God in infinite grace constructed the circle of religion around Himself. Furthermore, being out of harmony with God, man, as a sinner, has lost the rhythm of his own spiritual life; he is full of discords and inner conflicts, law clashing with law and in consequence the deepest self falling a prey to these disruptive forces which attack it at its core. The very moment the prodigal leaves the Father's house he carries this fatal disorder within him, he is beside himself in principle, so that, when in bitter repentance he begins to realize his desperate condition, this is described as a "coming to himself." This, then, in the first place is "being lost," and to this in the first place addresses itself the task of the Son of Man. Hence its first part must of necessity be a "seeking" of the sinner. And the "seeking" must be such an act as will be able to undo the "being lost." We should, therefore, take a far too superficial view of it, were we to confine it to the bare effort at approach, or perhaps even to the search for locating the sinner, as the figure, taken by itself, might tempt us to do. No, the finding is not the mere discovery, it is the actual bringing back to God, something by which the sinner is restored to the blessed reality of what God is to him and he is to God: "And when he came to himself he said, I will arise and go to my Father." Are we not made to feel by this, that not first in the saving but already in the finding begins the uniqueness of the

Savior's work, that which differentiates it from any finding
that we can do, however glorious the latter may be in itself.
For, after all, our finding of a man can be only preparatory
to his becoming partaker of salvation. In the case of Christ it
is identical with the saving act itself. Yea already the seeking
is a part of the finding, because with unfailing certainty and
directness the feet and the arms of the Savior move to the
point where the saving embrace is accomplished. In the last
analysis the difference between this and our part appears due
to the difference between Christ as God and ourselves as
mere human instrumentalities. To be found by Jesus is to be
saved for the simple reason that in his Person God Himself
restores the lost contact, gathers up the cords of life into His
own bosom, and throws about us the circle of his divine
beatitude, so that our soul, like a star in its native course,
once more moves around Him, and knows no other law or
center. So far as Christ was a preacher He preached with the
voice of God, and in his message salvation was not merely
potential but incarnate. He silently takes this for granted in
his whole treatment of sinners, when He deals with them
sovereignly in the supreme issues of life and death. In a word
He saves as God saves. On this ground, and on this ground
only, can we understand why so seldom in the matter of
salvation He points beyond Himself to God, but constantly
places his own Person in the center of the sinner's field of
vision, so as to focus belief and trust and hope and surrender
and attachment in Himself. Consequently it is true not only
in the abstractly logical, but in the most realistic, one might
almost say in the local sense, that where Jesus is, there is

salvation, and away from Him there is none. As Here
rebuked the disciples in the storm, because they forgot this
fact, and feared that with Him on board they still might
perish, even so He requires of us that in every tempest of life
we shall be tranquil, because our ship carries Him. Was it
not so in this very case of Zacchaeus? Because He had
entered, salvation in Him and through Him had entered into
the publican's house.

Salvation, however, according to our Lord's teaching is
not exhausted by restoring the sinner to a sense of the
realities of his appurtenance to God. There is another
equally indispensable side to it. What this is we may learn by
considering the second element that enters into the state of
"being lost." "To be lost" is more than to be missing to
God. It has also the passive, even more terrible sense of
"being ruined," "given up to destruction." The former sense
remains within the sphere of the negative it describes what is
absent from the sinner's state; this other sense is positive,
denoting the presence of something dreadful there. If our
Lord's discourse dwells chiefly, and with a noticeable
predilection, on the first aspect of the matter, this is perhaps
due to the vividness with which by very reason of the
concrete, detailed picture of what is wanting, the glorious
realities of religion are brought out. The rule that we do not
clearly visualize a thing until through its departure and its
consequent failure to function it recalls its image to our
mind, is here put to practical use. Strange to say, the face of
religion appears in our Lord's teaching most clearly in the
form of a description of its opposite. "In my father's house

there is bread enough and to spare, while I perish with hunger"—what glowing words could have more powerfully expressed the blessedness of spiritual satisfaction near the heart of God than this pitiful cry of want! There is a lesson for us in this. We shall never succeed in impressing men, untouched by grace, with the riches and glory of religion, until we learn from Jesus to hold up to them the mirror of their sin and destitution. To say that there is no experience of redemption without the knowledge of sin sounds like a truism; perhaps it will appear less so, if we go one step farther and add, that there is, as things are, no proper, no deep knowledge either of religion or of redemption than through the sorrowful journey into the far country of famine and husks. But, while fourth is obvious reason the greater part of Jesus' teaching on the lost is concerned with the first aspect of their state, it would be wrong to infer that the other side only slightly or perfunctorily figured in his mind. The contrary is true. The subject possessed for Him such a fearful reality, that, except on the most solemn and imperative occasions. He hesitated to contemplate or draw it into the glare of open speech. It is nonetheless there with the ominous darkness of untold, nay unspeakable things spread over it like a semi-opaque curtain. To be sure, it is something future, but this only deepens the gloom that covers it. It is born of the womb of the judgment. "Broad is the way that leads to perdition" and the lost are those walking on it. Only this should not be taken to mean that the loss contemplated is purely future. It overhangs and envelops the sinner even in this life. As the narrow path to the city of God, notwithstanding its straightness, is already bordered with some of the flowers and fruits of paradise, so the highway to the land of destruction, in spite of its seeming delights, has long stretches of shadow from the storm cloud that is seen to thicken at the end. Even in this ultimate, more perilous, sense it is not sufficient to say that the sinner will suffer loss in the last day; according to the conception of Jesus he in principle is already lost. We feel something of the awful import conveyed, when in his high-priestly prayer the Savior declares: "Holy Father, I kept them in thy name which Thou hast given me; and I guarded them, and none of them was lost except the son of perdition." For, although Judas's in degree was altogether beyond comparison, it was not in substance different from each sin of every one of us. Except for the intervention of God no one has ever turned back on the broad way to perdition. Here in verily is seen the uttermost divine grace, that Christ seeks and saves from the plight of that despair. If our eyes delight to see Him as the friendly Shepherd on the trail of the lost sheep, let us not turn our looks away from Him in this more solemn occupation of rescuing the lost from the judgment. Yea let us see Him in the darkness of the cross. For this part of the saving also takes place in no other way than the more gentle one we have already considered. Here too He not merely announces or promises the salvation, but carries it in his own Person. He is the impersonation of the God who pronounces the judgment and of the God who sovereignly takes it away, the one who bears our curse, and, while bearing it, speaks peace to our souls. For this cause He came to the cross, that He might be able to act for God in this solemn, anticipated judgment through which every sinner passes. When He speaks of sin and pardon and escape, the voice is the voice of God and the arms stretched underneath us are the everlasting arms of the Almighty Himself.

There is one other point on which we must briefly touch before closing. The text represents the object of the saving in the impersonal form as "that which was lost." The impersonal form of expression carries with it a generalizing effect. It amounts practically to "whatsoever is lost." The motive in our Lord's mind for this is not difficult to discover. A murmuring populace had excluded the class of publicans from the sphere that was worthy of his attention. To this Jesus replies with the emphatic declaration, that all that is lost falls under the legitimate scope of his task, that, since the very fact of salvation is evoked by there being lost one's, no exception can be allowed from its grace on the mere ground that the object appears lost. Within the realm of sin distinctions between class and class or degree and degree of sinners become obliterated. In comparison with the one tremendous fact of sin as such they dwindle into insignificance, or if there is any differentiation observable it assumes rather the opposite, paradoxical form of those taking the precedence, in whom, by reason of excessive sinfulness and most poignant sense of guilt, salvation's opportunity for magnifying itself is increased. The harlots and publicans enter first into the kingdom of God. But we should surely misinterpret this, if we took it to mean that

Jesus, after precisely the same fashion seeks and saves each single one that is lost. Grace knows no jealousy except for the honor of God. With wide generousness, such as only a renewal of heart can give, it yearns and prays for the ingathering of many. Nonetheless, when as saved sinners we place ourselves individually before God, who would not feel it as a denial of salvation itself to forget that pointedly and with a special mysterious determination the search, which in its issue placed him among the saved, was instituted and pursued for him on the part of God and Christ? Let us not from hyper-altruistic squeamishness allow ourselves to gloss this over, for, besides withholding from God the glory which is his due in it, we should lose for ourselves the most precious portion of God's saving grace. It is not as if Christ at random wandered through this world on the chance of finding someone upon whom to exercise his power of salvation. With reference to each one of the children of God there was with Him from the beginning a unique compassion, a personalized love, and in result of this a singleness and determination of purpose, that imparted to his seeking of the least one of us the glory of a private inclusion in the intimate circle of God's saved ones. Of such seeking Jesus was conscious, and with all the wideness of his compassionate heart, which no world of sinners could overcrowd, He was not ashamed to acknowledge the gracious privileges and distinctions that pertained to the Lord's people or to any individual child of God. On this very occasion He gave expression to them in the words: "Inasmuch as he also is a son of Abraham," words which trace back the blessed issue of Zacchaeus' encounter with Jesus to the covenantal promise made ages before to the patriarch, and ultimately to the sovereign election of which this promise was the outcome. It is with this as it is with the Pauline statement: no more than one can say, "Who loved me and gave Himself for me," is it possible to say. Who sought me and saved me, except by a profound faith in the elective purpose as the ultimate cause of the personal inheritance of salvation. Now what in conclusion" are the lessons that we, seekers of the salvation of others, ought to draw from this episode in our Lord's life? They are chiefly two, and I shall indicate them with the briefest of words. The first relates to the specialized character we as servants of Christ ought to make our work to bear. If his procedure is normative for us—and who would deny this? then all our seeking and saving, that is, all our religious endeavor, ought to carry the image and superscription of Christ's. And here the salient point is undoubtedly this, that the purpose, the goal of seeking and saving were for our Lord pronouncedly religious. Seeking and saving meant for Him, before aught else, seeking and saving for God. It had no humanitarian or world-improving purpose apart from this. It began with the thought of God and ended there. For that He came. And at that we should aim. This conception will not narrow our work any more than it did his, it will only centralize it. Beginning there we shall find that everything else will follow that ought to follow. Was it not so in the case of Zacchaeus? Once Jesus had entered his house with salvation, he could not help taking his stand as one morally and socially reconstructed before the crowd of detractors: "Behold, Lord, the half of my goods I give to the poor; and if I have wrongfully exacted aught of any man, I restore fourfold." Provided the precious nard of religion be poured into it, no vessel is unworthy. But, on the other hand, the finest flagon of the world, when bearing a false trademark, and under the guise of religion offering some inferior substitute, has no proper place in the service of Christ. It belongs to the hidden things of shame which Paul had discarded. No servant of Christ should touch it. And even though other things be not positively deceitful or harmful in themselves, our duty of bringing salvation is so transcendently important and exacting that the Christian minister cannot afford to lose time or energy over them. The second lesson relates to what our specifically religious task of saving should centrally consist in. It may all be summed up in the simple formula, to bring Christ to men and men to Christ. It sounds simple, but is in reality a most difficult and most delicate task. No painter portraying face upon canvass ever used more exquisite art than is his who is preaching the gospel succeeds in so delineating the face of Christ as to make Him lookout with his immortal Savior eyes straight and deep into the hearts of sinners. Let your one concern be to bring the two together in the house where salvation is needed, and having led the Savior in, go thou out and shut the door silently behind thee. I tell you they shall not come out thence until salvation has done its perfect work.

IV. "Rabboni!"

John 20:16:

"Jesus saith unto her, Mary. She turneth herself and
saith unto Him in Hebrew, Rabboni; which is to
say, Master."

Our text takes us to the tomb of the risen Lord, on the first Sabbath morning of the New Covenant. It is impossible for us to imagine a spot more radiant with light and joy than was this immediately after the resurrection. Even when thinking ourselves back into the preceding moments, while as yet to the external eye there was nothing but the darkness of death, our anticipation of what we know to be about to happen floods the scene with a twilight of supernatural splendor. The sepulcher itself has become to us prophetic of victory; we seem to hear in the expectant air the wingbeat of the descending angels, come to roll away the stone and announce to us: "The Lord is risen indeed!" Besides this, we have learned to read the story of our Lord's life and death so as to consider the resurrection it's only possible outcome, and this has to some extent dulled our sense for the startling character of what took place. We interpret the resurrection in terms of the atoning cross, and easily forget how little the disciples were as yet prepared for doing the same. And so it requires an effort on our part to understand sympathetically the state of mind they brought to the morning of this day. Nevertheless we must try to enter into their thoughts and feelings, if for no other reason, for this, that something of the same fresh marvel and gladness that subsequently came to them may fill our hearts also. Whether we maybe able to explain it or not, the Gospel tells us, that, notwithstanding the emphatic prediction by the Savior of his death and resurrection, they had but little remembrance of these words, and drew from them no practical support or comfort in the sorrow that overwhelmed them. In part this may have been due to the fact of our Lord's having only predicted and not fully explained these tremendous events. At anyrate the circumstance shows that there is need of a deeper faith than that of mere acquaintance with and consent to external statements of truth, when the dread realities of life and death assail us. Dare we say that we ourselves should have proved stronger in such a trial, if over against all that mocked our hope we had been able to place no more than a dimly remembered promise? Let us thank God that, when we ourselves enter into the valley of the shadow of death, we have infinitely more than a promise to stay our hearts upon, that ours is the fulfilment of the promise, the fact of the resurrection, nay the risen Lord Himself present with rod and staff beside us.

Supplementing the account of John with the statements of the other Evangelists, we gain the following conception of the course of events previous to what the text relates. A small company of women went out at early dawn towards the garden, carrying the spices prepared as a last offering to honor Jesus. From among these Mary Magdalene in the eagerness of her desire to reach the place, ran forward, and discovered before the others that the stone had been rolled away. Without awaiting the arrival of her companions she hastens back to tell Peter and John what she supposed to be true: "They have taken away the Lord out of the tomb." Roused from the lethargy of their grief by this startling announcement the Apostles immediately went to the place, and by their own observation verified Mary's report. John came first, but merely looked into the tomb. Peter, who

followed, entered in, and beheld the linen cloths lying and
the napkin that was upon the Savior's head rolled up and put
by itself. Then entered in John also and saw and believed.
For as yet they knew not the Scripture that He must rise
again from the dead. Their eyes were so holden that the true
explanation never occurred to them. Perplexed, but not
moved from a despairing state of mind, they returned to
their abode.

Mary must have followed the Apostles at a distance when
these came in haste to see for themselves. We find her
standing without the tomb weeping. Is it not remarkable
that, while both John and Peter departed, Mary remained?
Although the same hopeless conclusion had forced itself
upon her, yet it could not induce her to leave. In her mind it
only intensified a thousand times the purpose with which she
had come. How striking an illustration of the Savior's word
that much forgiveness creates Abounding love! But may we
not believe that still something else reveals itself in this?
Mary's attitude towards Jesus, more perhaps than any other
disciple's seems to have been characterized by that simple
dependence, which is but the consciousness of an ever
present need. It was a matter of faith, as much as of love,
that made her differ at this time from the others. Unmixed
with further motives, the recognition of Jesus as the only
refuge from sin and death filled her heart. In a measure, of
course. He had been this to the others also. But whilst to
them He stood for many other things in addition, the
circumstances under which she had become attached to Him
made Mary's soul the mirror of saving faith pure and simple.

And because she was animated by this fundamental spiritual impulse, drawing her to the Savior more irresistible than affection or sorrow could have done, therefore she could not but continue seeking Him, even though unable for the moment to do aught else than weep near his empty tomb. In vain does Calvary proclaim that the Lord is dead, in vain does the tomb declare that He has been buried, in vain does the absent stone suggest that they have taken Him away— this threefold witness will not convince Mary that He has gone out of her life forever. And why? Because in the depth of her being there was an even more emphatic witness which would not be silenced but continued to protest that she must receive Him back, since He is her Savior. Contact, communion with Christ had become to her the vital breath of her spiritual life; to admit that the conditions rendering this possible had ceased to exist would have meant for her to deny salvation itself. There is, it is true, apathetic incongruousness between the absoluteness of this desire and the futile form in which for the moment she thought it could be satisfied. In the last analysis what was she doing but seeking a lifeless body, in order that by caring for it and feeling near it she might still the longing of a living faith? Suppose she had received what she sought, would not in the next moment the other deeper desire have reasserted itself for that in Him which it was absolutely beyond the power of a dead Jesus to give her? Still, however incongruous the form of expression, it was an instinct to which an outward reality could not fail to correspond. It arose out of a primary need, for which provision must exist somewhere, if redemption exists at all. Though unaware of the resurrection as a fact, she had laid hold upon the supreme principle from which its necessity flows. Once given the intimate bond of faith between a sinner and his Savior, there can be no death to such a relationship. Mary, in her simple dependence on Jesus, had risen to the point where she sought in Him life and sought it ever more abundantly. To her faith He was Conqueror over death long before He issued from the grave. She was in rapport with that spiritual aspect, that quickening quality of his Person, of which the resurrection is the sure consequence Here at bottom lies the decisive issue for everyone as regards the attitude to be assumed towards this great fact. Ultimately, stripped of all accidentals, the question resolves itself into this: What means Christ for us? For what do we need Him? If we have learned to know ourselves guilty sinners, destitute of all hope and life in ourselves, and if we have experienced that from Him came to us pardon, peace and strength, will it not sound like mockery in our ears, if somebody tells us, that it does not matter, whether Jesus rose from the dead on the third day? It is of the very essence of saving faith that it clamors for facts, facts to show that the heavens have opened, that the tide of sinful nature has been reversed, the guilt of sin expiated, the reign of death destroyed and life and immortality brought to light. And because this is the insuppressible cry of faith, what else should faith do, when it sees doubt and unbelief emptying the Gospel of the living Christ, what else should it do but stand outside weeping and

repeating the plaint: They have taken away my Lord and I
know not where they have laid Him?

But, although these things were in principle present in
Mary's heart, she did not at that moment perceive the pledge
of hope contained in them. Her grief was too profound to
leave room for introspection. It even hid from her vision the
objective evidence of the resurrection that lay around her.
Worse than this, she turned what was intended to help her
into an additional reason for unbelief. But who of us shall
blame her? Have not we ourselves under as favorable
circumstances made the mistake of nourishing our unbelief
on what was meant to be food for our faith? Do we not all
remember occasions when we stood outside the grave of our
hopes weeping, and did not perceive the hand stretched out
to prepare us by the very thing we interpreted as sorrow for
a higher joy? From Mary's experience let us learn to do
better. What the Lord expects from us at such seasons is not
to abandon ourselves to unreasoning sorrow, but trustingly
to look sorrow in the face, to scan its features, to search for
the help and hope, which, as surely as God is our Father,
must be there. In such trials there can be no comfort for us
so long as we stand outside weeping. If only we will take the
courage to fix our gaze deliberately upon the stern
countenance of grief, and enter unafraid into the darkest
recesses of our trouble, we shall find the terror gone,
because the Lord has been there before us, and, coming out
again, has left the place transfigured, making out of it by the
grace of his resurrection a house of life, the very gate of
heaven.

This was just what happened to Mary. Not forever could she stand weeping, forgetful of what went on around her. "As she wept she looked into the tomb, and she beholdeth two angels in white sitting one at the head and one at the feet, where the body of Jesus had lain." It was a step in the right direction that she roused herself from her inaction. Still, what strikes us as most characteristic in this state-ment is its implying that even the vision of angels did not sufficiently impress her to raise the question, to what the appearance of these celestial messengers might be due. Probably this was the first time she had come in direct contact with the supernatural in that particular form. The place was doubtless charged with the atmosphere of mystery and wonder angels bring with themselves when entering into our world of sense. And yet no tremor seems to have run through her, no feeling of awe to have made her drawback. A greater blindness to fact is here than that which made her miss the sign of the empty grave. What more convincing evidence of the truth of the resurrection could have been offered than the presence of these two angels, silently, reverently, majestically sitting where the body of Jesus had lain? Placed like the Cherubim on the mercy seat, they covered between themselves the spot where the Lord had reposed, and flooded it with celestial glory. It needed no voice of theirs to proclaim that here death had been swallowed up in victory. Ever since the angels descended into this tomb the symbolism of burial has been radically changed. From this moment onward every last resting place where the bodies of believers are laid is a furrow in that great harvest field of Christ whence heaven draws upward into light each seed sunk into it, whence Christ himself was raised, the first fruits of them that sleep.

Let us not overlook, however, that Mary's disregard of the angels revealed in a most striking form something good also, to-wit: her intense preoccupation with the one thought of finding the Lord. For Him she had been looking into the tomb. He not being there, it was empty to her view, though filled with angelic glory. She would have turned aside without speaking, had not the angels of their own accord spoken to her: "Woman, why weepest thou?" These words were meant as an expression of sympathy quite natural in beings wont to rejoice over repenting sinners. But in this question there is at the same time a note of wonder at the fact that she should be weeping at all. To the mind of the angels the resurrection was so real, so self-evident, that they could scarcely understand how to her it could be otherwise. They felt, as it were, the discord between the songs of joy with which their own world was jubilant, and this sound of weeping coming out of a world of darkness and despair. "Woman, why weepest thou?" Tears would be called for indeed, hadst thou found Him in the tomb, but not at a time like this, when heaven and earth unite in announcing: He is risen in glory, the King of life!

Mary's answer to the angels shows that neither their sympathy nor their wonder had succeeded in piercing her sorrow. "She saith unto them. Because they have taken away my Lord, and I know not where they have laid Him." These

are almost the identical words in which she had informed
Peter and John of her discovery of the empty tomb. Still as
light change appears. To the Apostles she had said "the
Lord" and "we know not." To the angels it is "my Lord"
and "I know not." In this is revealed once more her intense
sense of proprietorship in Jesus. In that sense the angels
could not have appropriated Him for themselves. They
might hail Him as their matchless King, but to Mary He was
even more than this, her Lord, her Savior, the One who had
sought and saved and owned her in her sins.

Having given this answer to the angels she turned herself
backward and beheld Jesus standing, and knew not that it
was Jesus. No explanation is added of the cause of this
movement. It matters little. Our interest at this stage of the
narrative belongs not to what Mary but to what Jesus did.
On his part the encounter was surely not accidental but
intended. He had witnessed her coming once and again, her
weeping, her bending over the tomb, her answer to the
angels, and had witnessed not only these outward acts, but
also the inward conflict by which her soul was torn. And He
appears precisely at the point where his presence is
required, because all other voices for conveying to her the
gladsome tidings have failed. He had been holding Himself in
readiness to become in his own Person the preacher of the
Gospel of life and hope to Mary. There is great comfort for
us in this thought that, however dim our conscious faith and
the sense of our salvation, on the Lord's side the fountain of
grace is never closed, its connection with our souls never
interrupted provided there be the irrepressible demand for

his presence. He cannot. He will not deny Himself to us. The first person to whom He showed Himself alive after the resurrection was a weeping woman, who had no greater claim upon Him than any simple penitent sinner has. No eye except that of the angels had as yet rested upon His form. The time was as solemn and majestic as that of the first creation when light burst out of chaos and darkness. Heaven and earth were concerned in this event; it was the turning point of the ages. Nor was this merely objectively so Jesus felt Himself the central figure in this new-born universe, He tasted the exquisite joy of one who had just entered upon an endless life in the possession of new powers and faculties such as human nature had never known before. Would it have been unnatural, had He sought some quiet place to spend the opening hour of this new unexplored state in communion with Father? Can there be any room in his mind for the humble ministry of consolation required by Mary? He answers these questions Himself. Among all the voices that hailed his triumph no voice appealed to Him like this voice of weeping in the garden. The first appearance of the risen Lord was given to Mary for no other reason than that she needed Him first and needed Him most. And what more appropriate beginning could have been set for his ministry of glory than this very act? Nothing could better convince us, that in his exalted state He retains for us the same tender sympathy, the same individual affection as He showed during the days of his flesh. It is well for us to know this, because otherwise the dread impression of his majesty might tend to hinder our approach to Him. Who of us has not at some time of communion with the Savior felt the overwhelming awe that seized the seer on Patmos, so that we could not utter our prayer, until He laid his hand upon us and said: Fear not. We should be thankful, then, for the grace of Christ which has so arranged it, that between his rising from the dead and his departure for heaven a season of forty days was interposed, a transition period, helping, as it were, the feebleness of our faith in the act of apprehending his glory. Perhaps the Lord for the same reason also intentionally placed his meeting with Mary at the threshold of his resurrection life. Like other acts recorded in the Fourth Gospel this act rises above the momentary situation and acquires a symbolic significance, enlarging before our eyes until it reveals Him in his priestly ministration conducted from the throne of glory.

However not the fact only of his showing Himself to Mary, but likewise the manner of it claims our attention. When first beholding Him she did not know the Lord, and even after his speech she still supposed Him to be the gardener. The chief cause for this may have lain in the change which had taken place in Him when the mortal put on immortality. Now behold with what exquisite tact the Lord helps her to restore the broken bond between the image her memory retained of Him and that new image in which henceforth He would walk through her life and hold converse with her spirit. Even these first words: "Woman why weepest thou? Whom seekest thou?" though in form scarcely differing from the question of the angels, go far beyond the latter in their power to reach Mary's heart. In

the word "woman" with which He addresses her speaks all
the majesty of one who felt Himself the Son of God in
power by resurrection from the dead. It is a prelude to the
still more majestic, "Touch me not" spoken soon
afterwards. And yet in the words, "Why weepest thou?
Whom seekest thou?" He extends to her that heart-
searching sympathy, which at a single glance can read and
understand the whole secret of her sorrow. He knew that
such weeping results only there where one who is more than
father or mother has been taken away. And how
instantaneous the effect these words produced! Though she
still supposes him the gardener, she takes for granted that he
at least could not have taken the body with evil intent, that
he will not refuse to restore it: "Sir, if thou hast borne Him
hence, tell me where thou hast laid Him, and I will take Him
away." A certain response to his sympathy is also shown in
this, that three times she refers to Jesus as "Him" deeming it
unnecessary to mention his name. Thus in the way she met
the gardener there was already the beginning resumption of
the bond of confidence between her and the Lord. And thus
Jesus found the way prepared for making Himself known to
her in a most intimate manner. "Jesus saith unto her 'Mary.'
She turneth and saith unto Him, 'Rabboni'. "It happened all
in a moment, and by a simple word, and yet in this one
moment Mary's world was changed for her. She had in that
instant made the transition from hopelessness because Jesus
was absent, to fullness of joy because Christ was there. We
may well despair of conveying by any process of exposition
the meaning of these two words. This is speech the force of

which can only be felt. And it will be felt by us in proportion
as we clearly remember some occasion when the Lord spake
a similar word to us and drew from us a similar cry of
recognition. Doubtless much of the magical effect of Jesus'
word was due to the tone in which He spoke it. It was a tone
calling to her remembrance the former days of closest
fellowship. This was the voice that He alone could use, the
same voice that had once commanded the demons to depart
from her, and to which ever since she had been wont to
listen for guidance and comfort. By using it He meant to
assure her, that, whatever transformation had taken place,
there could be and would be no change in the intimate,
personal character of their relationship. And Mary was quick
to apprehend this. The Evangelist takes pains to preserve for
us the word she uttered in its original Aramaic form,
because he would have us understand that it meant more at
this moment than could be conveyed by the ordinary
rendering of "Teacher" or "Master." "Rabboni" has a
special untranslatable significance. It was the personal
response to the personal "Mary," to all intents a proper
name no less than the other. By speaking it Mary consciously
re-entered upon the possession of all that as Rabboni He had
meant to her. Only one thing she had yet to learn, for
teaching her which the Lord did not deem even this unique
moment too joyful or sacred. In the sudden revulsion from
her grief Mary would have given some external expression
to the tumult within by grasping and holding Him. But He
restrained her, saying: "Touch me not, for I am not yet
ascended unto the Father; but go unto my brethren and say

to them, I ascend unto my Father and your Father, and my
God and your God." At first sight these words may seem a
contrast to those immediately preceding. And yet no
mistake could be greater than to suppose that the Lord's sole
or chief purpose was to remind her of the restrictions which
henceforth were to govern the intercourse between Himself
and her. His intention was much rather to show that the
desire for a real communion of life would soon be met in a
new and far higher way than was possible under the
conditions of local earthly nearness. "Touch me not" does
not mean: Touch is too close a contact to be henceforth
permissible; it means: the provision for the highest, the ideal
kind of touch has not been completed yet: "I am not yet
ascended to my Father." His words were denial of the
privilege she craved only as to the form and moment in
which she craved it; in their larger sense they are a pledge, a
giving, not a withholding of Himself from her. The great
event of which the resurrection is the first step has not yet
fulfilled itself; it requires for its completion the ascent to the
Father. But when once this is accomplished then all
restrictions will fall away, and the desire to touch that made
Mary stretch forth her hand shall be gratified to its full
capacity. The thought is not different from that expressed in
the earlier saying to the disciples: "Ye shall see me because I
go to the Father." There is a seeing, a hearing, a touching,
first made possible by Jesus' entrance into heaven and by the
gift of the Spirit dependent on that entrance. And what He
said to Mary He commissioned her to repeat to his brethren,
that they also might be taught to view the event in its proper

perspective. May we not fitly close our study of the text with reminding ourselves that we too are included among the brethren to whom He desired these tidings to be brought? Before this He had never called the disciples by this name, as He had never until now so suggestively identified Himself with them by speaking of "your Father and my Father" and "your God and my God." We are once more assured that the new life of glory, instead of taking Him from us, has made us in a profounder sense his brethren and his Father our Father. Though, unlike Mary and the disciples, we have not been privileged to behold Him in the body, yet together with the believers of all ages we have an equal share in what is far sweeter and more precious, the touch through faith of his heavenly Person for which the appearances after the resurrection were but a preparation. Let us then not linger at the tomb, but turn our faces and stretch our hands upwards into heaven, where our life is hid with Him in God, and whence He shall also come again to show Himself to us as He did to Mary, to make us speak the last great "Rabboni," which will spring to the lips of all the redeemed, when they meet their Savior in the early dawn of that eternal Sabbath that awaits the people of God.

V. The More Excellent Ministry

2 Corinthians 3:18:

"But we all, with unveiled face, beholding as in a
mirror the glory of the Lord, are transformed into
the same image from glory to glory, even as from
the Lord, the Spirit."

In his second letter of Paul to the Church at Corinth is marked by a pronounced polemic strain. In this respect it somewhat resembles the Epistle to the Galatians. In each instance a serious crisis in the life of the church had evoked it. It is further common to both writings that in certain passages the polemic assumes a sharply personal character. In neither case is this due to any temperamental difficulty on Paul's part to control his outraged feelings, although even if this had been so, much could have been said in excuse of the Apostle. His opponents had certainly not been sparing in personalities. He had been represented as a deceiver, as one who preached himself and praised himself. It had been charged that in his quasi-Apostolic authority he lorded it over the church, employed his usurped power for casting down instead of for building up, and that, in spite of all this bluff and bluster of prestige, he lacked the ability to make good his pretensions, being indeed weighty and strong in his letters, but weak in his bodily presence, and in his speech, of no account. The insinuation had been made that Paul himself was aware of the hollowness of his claims, because he would not take from the church the support to which, if a true Apostle, he ought to have felt himself entitled. He had been held up as a man who by his fickleness, his yea yea, nay nay, betrayed the duplicity of his position. The Apostle had not even been spared that meanest of all aspersions —that he was spending money collected for the poor saints in Judea on his own person. His sincerity as a minister of the truth had been called into question. It was charged that, while aware of his subordination to the original Apostles, he was disloyal to them, and substituted for their gospel an entirely different one spun out of his own mind. Thus the truth of the very substance of his preaching was challenged. In this respect again a certain resemblance to the tactics of his Galatian opponents may be observed. The charge in both instances was that he preached "a different gospel." Nevertheless the point of attack had been some what shifted. In Galatia the main question had been that of salvation with or without the law. Here in Corinth, on the other hand, the controversy raged around Paul's teaching concerning the Christ. It was with another Jesus that his opponents had approached the Corinthians. No effort had been spared to prove this the true Jesus, by the side of whom the Christ of Paul's preaching was a pure figment of the imagination. Suspicion had been cast on the source of his knowledge of the Savior on the ground that the visions through which it was obtained belonged to the class of wild, fantastic experiences, and that these marked Paul as one beside himself, not merely in this one point, but in the entire tone and temper of his religious life. The exalted, spiritual, heavenly nature, in which his gospel clothed the glorified Christ, was construed as convincing proof of the darkness and incomprehensibleness of the Apostle's message. He preached a Gospel that was veiled. Andover against these elusive and intangible things had been placed the palpable institutions of the Mosaic Covenant, carrying with them the demand for a Messiah correspondingly substantial and realistic in his make-up. This is but an early illustration of the principle which from that time onward has shaped all forms of teaching in the Church. For in each instance the view about the method of salvation is reflected in the conception of the Savior. A certain Gospel requires a certain kind of Christ, and a certain type of Christ a certain Gospel.

It might have seemed as if the attack upon the Apostle had therewith reached its logical conclusion and could not possibly go farther. Still this was not the case. With a curious retroversive movement the issue had been carried back from this point to the question of the personality of Paul, with this difference only—it was now his dignity in office that had been assailed. Paul's office as such was made out to be mean and contemptible. Such a Christ and such a cause could engage one who labored for them only in the weakest and most ignoble kind of service. Paul was not permitted to escape the immemorial stigma reflected upon the minister from the apparent foolishness and weakness of the cross. And the Apostle was sensitive, if anywhere, on this point of the nobility and glory of his office. Moral aspersions against his character he might, had it not been for fear of danger to the churches, have passed by as unworthy of notice. But the pride of office was stronger in him than the sense of personal honor. And thus it happens that we are indebted to these disturbers of the Corinthian church, whose names have long been forgotten, for an encomium upon the Gospel service, which for power and splendor has no equal in the records of Christian apology. It deserves to be placed beside the song of triumph in the eighth chapter of the Epistle to the Romans. As there the Apostle is carried on the crest-wave of assurance of salvation, so here he moves with

the full tide of enthusiasm over the excellence of his calling.
The very words are, as it were, baptized in the glory of
which they speak.

Let us briefly examine the several elements that enter
into this high consciousness. The form of argument which
Paul adopts is evidently determined by the method of his
detractors. At the climax of their calumny they had
concentrated their attack on the meanness and weakness of
his message. Consequently he chooses to defend himself on
the same basis by arguing from the glory of the message to
the distinction of the bearer. While thus adjusted to the
manner of attack, this method was also in keeping with
Paul's innate modesty, still further refined by grace. But
there was another tactical motive besides. Paul recognized
that by thus approaching the subject a more substantial title
to official prestige could be made out than in any other way,
such, perhaps, as calling attention to outward results. After
all it is not so much by what the minister contributes of
himself to the cause of Christ, but rather by what he is
enabled to draw out and utilize from the divine resources,
that his office and work will be tested. It is not chiefly the
question whether we are strong in the cause, but whether
the cause is strong in and through us. And herein lies the
practical value of the argument in its application to the
servants of Christ under all conditions. If Paul had staked the
issue on the personal factor, then there could be in his
testimony but little comfort and encouragement for others,
for there are not many Pauls. Now that the subject is dealt
within the other way the Apostle's words contain something

enheartening for you and me and the simplest, obscurest bearer of the Gospel. We are too often told at the present day that the official, professional distinction of the minister is a matter of the past, that it has become purely a question of what is called personal magnetism whether he shall earn successor failure. Paul certainly was far from this opinion. To be sure, to such things as ecclesiastical position or rank he would hardly have attributed much importance. Even the difference between the Apostolate and other forms of service in the Church seems scarcely to enter into the reckoning here. But within the realm of the invisible and spiritual there remains such a thing as an intrinsic prestige. Paul is conscious of belonging to a veritable elite of the Spirit. I beg you to notice on how large a scale this thought is projected. It gives rise to the conception of a ministry of God's covenant, that is, a ministry identified with an all comprehensive dispensation of divine grace. Thus Moses was a minister of the Old and Paul is a minister of the New Covenant. To have such a Covenant ministry means to be identified with God in the most intimate manner, for the Covenant expresses the very heart of God's purpose. It means to be initiated into the holiest mysteries of redemption, for in the Covenant these are transacted. It means to be enrolled on the list of the great historic servants of God, for in the organism of the Covenant these are united and salute each other across the ages. It means to become a channel through which supernatural currents flow. In the Covenant the servant is, as it were, made part of the wonder-world of salvation itself. The Apostle has embodied this grandiose thought in a most striking figure. "Thanks be to God," he exclaims, "who always leadeth us in triumph in Christ." The onward march of the Gospel is a triumphal procession, God the victorious Conqueror, Paul a follower in God's train, burning the incense to his glory, making manifest the savor of his knowledge in every place!

What has been said so far applies to the ministry of the Covenant of Grace under both dispensations. It describes a glory common to Moses and Paul. The Apostle ungrudgingly recognizes that the Old Testament had its peculiar distinction. To be a prophet or priest of the God of Israel conferred greater honor than any secular prominence in the pagan history of the race. Even the ministration written and engraven on stones came with glory. This excellence of the Old Covenant found a symbolic expression in the light upon the face of Moses after his tarrying with God upon the mount, a light so intense that the children of Israel could not steadfastly look upon its radiance. Paul's purpose, however, is not to emphasize what the two dispensations have in common, but that in which the New surpasses the Old. Since the opponents had clothed their attack upon him in the invidious form of a comparison with the Mosaic administration, it was natural for him to take up the challenge and fight out the battle along the same line. Nonetheless the comparison, as followed up by Paul, is startling in its exceeding boldness. A more impressive disclosure of his exalted sense of office is scarcely conceivable. In order to feel the full force of this we ought to make clear to ourselves that not two single persons but

two pairs of persons are set over against each other. On the
one side stand God and Moses, the reflector of his glory, on
the other Christ and Paul, the reflector of his glory. It would
be interesting, but beside our present purpose, to consider
what it implies as to the nature and rank of Christ, that the
Apostle feels free simply to put Him on a line with God as a
fount and dispenser of glory in the New Covenant after no
different fashion than God was under the Old Covenant.
Without pursuing this further, we now wish to make the
point, that the comparison lies not between Moses and
Christ, but between Moses and Paul. Than Moses no greater
name was known in the annals of Old Testament
redemption. Prophet, priest, law-giver in one, he towers
high above all the others. And to Paul, the son of Israel, all
this wealth of sacred story gathered round the head of Moses
must have been a thousand times more impressive than it
can be to us. What an overwhelming sense then of the
greatness of his own ministry must Paul have possessed,
when he dared conceive the thought of being greater than
Moses! "Verily that which has been made glorious has been
made not-glorious in this respect by reason of the glory that
surpasseth."

The Apostle, however, does not give expression to this
lofty consciousness in an outburst of unreasoning
enthusiasm. He carefully specifies wherein the surpassing
excellence of his ministry above that of Moses consists. The
first point relates to the contrast between transitoriness and
eternity. Putting it in 'terms of the figure, Paul affirms that
the glory of the Old Covenant had to pass away, whereas

that of the New Covenant must remain. When Moses
descended from the mount his face shone with a refulgence
of the divine glory near which he had been permitted to
dwell for a season. But his face could not retain this
brightness for any length of time. It soon disappeared. Thus
what Moses stood for was glorious but lacked permanence.
The day was bound to come when its splendor would
vanish. On the other hand the New Covenant is final and
abiding. The times cannot outgrow, the developments of
history cannot antiquated it, it carries within itself the
pledge of eternity. But not only did such a difference
actually exist—both Moses and Paul were aware of the state
of things in each case. Moses was aware of it, for we are told
that he put the veil on his face for the purpose of hiding the
disappearance of the glory. And Paul was, since in pointed
contrast to this procedure, he professes to minister with
open face: "Not as Moses, who put a veil over his face." It
was further inevitable that in Paul's estimation the speedy
abrogation of Moses' work detracted from his glory as a
servant of the Covenant, and that, on the other hand, the
enduring character of his own work added greatly to the
honor wherewith Paul felt it clothed him and the satisfaction
he derived from it. Time, especially time with the wasting
power it acquires through sin, is the archenemy of all human
achievement. It kills the root of joy which otherwise belongs
to working and building. All things which the succeeding
generations of mankind have wrought in the course of the
ages succumb to its attacks. The tragic sense of this
accompanies the race at every step in its march through

history. It is like a pall cast over the face of the people's. In revealed religion through the grace of redemption it is in principle removed, yet not so that under the Old Covenant the dark shadow entirely disappears. The plaint of it is in Moses' own Psalm: "Thou turnest man to destruction — Thou carriest them away as with a flood." And something of this bitter taste of transitoriness enters even into the Old Testament consciousness of salvation. Now put over against this the triumphant song of life and assurance of immortality that fills the glorious, spacious days of the New Covenant, especially where first it issues from the womb of the morning bathed in the dew of imperishable youth. The note of futility and depression has disappeared, and in place of this the rapture of victory over death and decay, the exultant feeling of immersion in the atmosphere of eternity prevail. And this particularly communicated itself to the spirit in which the Covenant-ministration was performed. The joy of working in the dawn of the world to come quickens the pulse of all New Testament servants of Christ. Paul felt that the product of his labors, the output of his life, would shine with unfading splendor in the palace of God. Thus also the honor of being a fellow laborer of God first obtains its full rich meaning. It is the prerogative of God, the Eternal One, to work for eternity. As the King of the ages He discounts and surmounts all the intervening forces and barriers of time. He who is made to share in this receives the highest form which the divine image can assume in its reproduction in man. Neither things present nor things to come can conquer him. He reigns in life with God through Jesus Christ, his Lord.

In the second place, there is a difference operating to the advantage of Paul between the two ministries in regard to the measure of openness and clearness with which they are conducted. Moses ministered with covered, Paul J ministers with open, that is uncovered, face. As regards Moses this was that the children of Israel should not perceive the passing away of the glory underneath the veil. Not that Moses acted as a deceiver of his people. Paul means to say, that in receiving the glory, and losing it, and hiding its loss, he served the symbolic function of illustrating, in the first place, the glory of the Old Covenant, in the second place its transitoriness, and in the third place the ignorance of Israel in regard to what was taking place. The chief point of ignorance of the people related to the eclipse and abrogation their institutions would suffer. But the symbolism permits of being generalized, so as to include all the limitations of self-knowledge and self-understanding under which the Old Covenant labored. As a matter of fact Paul immediately afterwards extends it to Israel's entire reading of the law, that is, to Israel's self-interpretation and Scripture interpretation on a large scale. Ignorance as to the end would easily produce ignorance or imperfect understanding with reference to the whole order of things under which the people were living. Everything temporal and provisional, especially if it does not know itself as such, is apt to wear a veil. It often lacks the faculty of discriminating between what is higher and lower in its composition. Things that are ends and things that are mere means to an end are not always clearly separated. Every preparatory stage in the history of redemption can fully understand itself only in the light of that which fulfills it. The veil of the Old Covenant is lifted only in Christ. The Christian standpoint alone furnishes the necessary perspective for apprehending its place and function in the organism of the whole. So it came about that the Mosaic Covenant moved through the ages a mystery to itself and to its servants. According to Paul this tragical process reached its climax when Israel came face to face with Him who alone could interpret Israel to itself. It is not for us to unravel the web of self-misinterpretation and unbelief wrought by the Jews on the ancient loom previously to the appearance of Christ. Paul implies that both causes contributed to the sad result. There was an element of original guilt as well as of subsequent hardening involved. Their minds were blinded. The veil / was on the reading of Moses, but the veil was also on their hearts. And the Apostle's word still holds true: the veil remains until the present day. It can be taken away only when Israel shall turn to the Lord. Then, and not until then, that ghost of the Old Covenant which now accompanies Israel on its wandering through the ages, will vanish from its side. As a double gift of grace it will then receive the treasures of Moses and those of Paul from the hand of Christ.

It is in sharp contrast to all this that Paul describes his own mode of ministering under the New Covenant. He serves with unveiled face, and in this one figure all the openness, the self-intelligence, the transparency of his ministry find expression. The proclamation of the Word of the Gospel has left behind all the old reserve and restrictions and limitations under which Moses and his successors labored. Its ministers can now speak fully and freely and plainly The whole counsel of God. Paul glories in being able to do this. He uses great boldness of speech. There is nothing to withhold, nothing to conceal: the entire plan of redemption has been unfolded, the mystery hidden through the ages has been revealed, and there is committed to every ambassador of Christ an absolute message, no longer subject to change. Not the delicate procedure of the diplomat, who hides his aim, but the stately stepping forward of the herald who renders an authoritative pronouncement, characterizes his task to Paul's own mind. He discards all human artifice and invention, all insincere and undignified devices evidently employed by some at that time, as they are still not infrequently at the present time, to render the Gospel palatable to his hearers. He scorns, where principles are concerned, all compromise and concession: "Therefore, seeing we have this ministry, even as we obtained mercy, we faint not, but we have renounced the hidden things of shame, not walking in craftiness, nor handling the Word of God deceitfully, but by the manifestation of the truth commending ourselves to every man's conscience in the sight of God. "There is a straightforwardness, a simplicity in preaching, which is proportionate to the preacher's own faith in the absoluteness, and inherent truthfulness of his message. No shallow optimism about the adjustableness of Christianity to ever changing conditions, about its self-

rejuvenating power after apparent decline, can possibly
make up for a lack of this fundamental conviction. Unless we
are convinced with Paul that Christianity has a definable and
well defined message to bring, and are able to tell wherein it
consists, all our talk about its vitality or adaptability will
neither comfort ourselves nor deceive others. A thing is not
immortal because it is long-lived and dies hard. Only when
through all changes of time it preserves unaltered its essence
and source of power, can it be considered worthwhile as a
medicine for the sickness of the world. Something that needs
the constant use of cosmetics to keep up the appearance of
youth is a caricature of the Christianity of the New
Testament. Its case is worse than it imagines: it has not
merely passed its youth, but is in danger of losing its very
life.

In the next place, the greater distinction of the ministry
of the New Covenant springs from this that it is in the
closest conceivable manner bound up with the Person and
work of the Savior. It is a Christ dispensation in the fullest
sense of the word. What is possessed by the New Covenant
is not the glory of God as such, but the glory of God in the
face of Jesus Christ. Moses had a great vision on the
mountain, but Paul had a greater one, even as Moses himself
had a greater, when he stood with Elias on the New
Testament mount of transfiguration. Paul beholds the glory
of Christ as in a mirror, or, according to another rendering,
reflects it as a mirror. His entire task, both on its
communicative and on its receptive side, can be summed up
in his reflecting back the Christ-glory, caught by himself

unto others. To behold Christ and to make others behold Him is the substance of his ministry. All the distinctive elements of Paul's preaching relate to Christ, and bear upon their face his image and superscription. God is the Father of our Lord Jesus Christ. The Spirit is the Spirit of Christ. In the procuring of righteousness Christ is the one efficient cause. In Christ believers were chosen, called, justified, and will be glorified. To be converted is to die with Christ and to rise with Him. The entire Christian life, root and stem and branch and blossom, is one continuous fellowship with Christ. But to say that the Gospel is full of Christ is still too general a statement. What the Apostle affirms is that it is particularly the Gospel of the glory of Christ, and that, therefore, its ministry also has specifically to do with this. Now this is not a mere metaphorical way of speaking, as if it meant no more than that in every possible manner the Gospel preaching brings out and promotes the honor of the Savior. Paul intends it in a far more literal sense. The glory of Christ transmitted by his Gospel is an objective reality. It is that which effects the Savior's exalted state since the resurrection. While including the radiance of his external appearance, it is by no means confined to this. Paul reckons among this glory the whole equipment of grace and power and beauty, all the supernatural potencies and forces stored up in the risen Lord. It consists of energy no less than of splendor. Taken in this comprehensive, realistic sense, it is equivalent to the content of the Gospel, and determines the nature of its ministry. The rendering, "beholding as in a mirror" admirably fits into this representation. As a mirror is not an end in itself, but exists for the sake of what is seen through it, so the Gospel serves no other purpose than to bring men face to face with the glory of Christ. It is naught else but a tale of Christ, a Christ in words, the exact counterpart of Christ's Person and work in their glorious state. Because of the consciousness of this Paul felt himself greater than Moses, for the partial light that shone on the latter's face has now become omnipresent and fills the New Covenant. Under the Old Dispensation the servants of God saw only from afar the brightness of the Messiah's rising. Now He is visible from nearby, the One filling all in all, occupying the entire field of vision. The humblest of preachers surpasses in this respect the greatest of Old Testament evangelists. He carries a Gospel all fragrant and all radiant with Christ.

In the fourth place the excellence of the ministry of the New Covenant is seen in this—that it is a ministry of abundant forgiveness and righteousness. This aspect of it also is intimately connected with the glory of the Lord, although it requires a somewhat closer inspection to perceive this. It should be remembered that the glory possessed by Christ in heaven is, to Paul, the emphatic, never silent declaration of his absolute righteousness acquired during the state of humiliation. It sprang from his obedience and suffering and self-sacrifice in our stead. It is righteousness translated into the language of effect, the crown set upon his work of satisfaction. Consequently the servant of the New Covenant can attach his ministry of pardon and peace to the glory of Christ. Hence Paul in working out the comparison between

Moses and himself with special reference to the question of righteousness reduces the difference to terms of glory: "For if the ministry of condemnation is glory, much rather does the ministry of righteousness exceed in glory." In a broad sense the Old Testament was the economy of conviction of sin. The law revealed the moral helplessness of man, placed him under a curse, worked death. There was, of course. Gospel under and in the Old Covenant, but it was for its expression largely dependent on the silent symbolic language of altar and sacrifice and illustration. Under it the glory which speaks of righteousness was in hiding. In the New Covenant all this has been changed. The veil has been rent, and through it an unobstructed view is obtained of the glory of God on the face of Jesus Christ. And with this vision comes the assurance of atonement, satisfaction, access to God, peace of conscience, liberty, eternal life. For Paul the commission to proclaim these things constitutes no small part of the excellence of his task. As Jesus delighted in announcing release to the captives, in setting at liberty them that were bruised, in proclaiming the acceptable year of Jehovah, so Paul, even more because of the accomplishment of the redemptive work, rejoiced in the ministry of reconciliation. Beautiful to him upon the mountains were the feet of them that bring good tidings, that publish peace.

The fifth and principal reason why the service of the New Covenant excels in honor, Paul finds in this: that the Christ-glory is a living and self-communicating power, transforming both those who mediate it and those who receive it from glory to glory into the likeness of the Lord.

Paul here again has in mind the difference between Moses
and himself. Moses's own condition and appearance were
only externally and temporarily affected by the vision on the
mount. After a while his face became as before. And what he
was unable to retain for himself he was unable to
communicate unto others. Over against this the Apostle
places the two facts, first that the servants of the New
Covenant are integrally and permanently transformed by
beholding the image of the Lord, and second that they effect
a similar transformation in others to whom through their
ministry the knowledge of the glorified Savior comes. In its
first part this representation was doubtless connected with
the Apostle's personal experience. There had been a point in
his life at which the perception of the glorified Lord had
been for him attended with the most marvelous change it is
possible to undergo. The glory that shone around him on the
road to Damascus had in one moment, in the twinkling of an
eye, swept away all his old beliefs and ideals, his sinful
passion and pride, and made of him a new creature, to
whom the past things were like the faint memory of some
distant phase of existence. And what had happened there,
Paul had afterwards seen repeating itself thousands of times,
less conspicuously, to be sure, but not on that account less
truly, less miraculously. To express this aspect of his
ministry he employs the formula, that it is a ministry of the
Spirit, that is of the Holy Spirit, whereas that of Moses was
one of the letter. The Spirit stands for the living, energizing,
creative grace of God, the letter for the inability of the law
as such to translate itself into action. Now in saying that the

ministry of the New Covenant is a ministry of the glory of Christ and that it is a ministry of the Spirit Paul is not really affirming two different things but one and the same fact. The glory and the Spirit to him are identical. As we have seen the glory means the equipment, with supernatural power and splendor, of the exalted Christ. And this equipment, described from the point of view of its energizing source, consists of the Holy Spirit. It was at the resurrection that the Spirit in this high, unique sense was received by Him. There the Spirit transformed the Lord's human nature and made it glorious beyond conception. Besides this, the Spirit is with Christ in continuance as the indwelling principle, the element, as it were, in which the glorified life of the Savior is lived. We need not wonder, then, that a little later the Apostle gives almost paradoxical expression to this truth by declaring, "The Lord is the Spirit," and that we are transformed from "the Lord, the Spirit." This language is not, of course, intended to efface the distinction between the Second and the Third Persons of the Trinity, but simply serves to bring out the practical inseparableness of the exalted Christ and the Holy Spirit in the work of salvation. So we begin to understand at least a little of the mystery, how the glory of Christ can communicate itself to and reproduce itself in the believer and transform him. As Spirit-glory it cannot fail to do this, for it is of the nature of the Spirit so to act. Hence also we read elsewhere that Christ "became a quickening Spirit." The main point to be observed, however, is how all this adds to the high conception held by Paul about the honor of his ministry as compared with that of Moses. The minister of the law, the letter, can never taste that sweetest joy of seeing the message he brings incarnate and reincarnate itself in the lives of others. The minister of the New Covenant does taste of this joy: he writes with the Spirit of the living God in tables that are hearts of flesh. This means more than what we sometimes speak of and feel as pleasure in the consciousness of power set free or good accomplished. Paul undoubtedly knew this also, but to confine what he here describes to that would rob it of its most distinctive quality. Paul had the sensation of coming through his ministry into the closest touch with the forth-putting of the saving energy of God Himself. He was aware that to his preaching of the Gospel there belonged an invisible background, that at every step his presentation of the truth was accompanied by a ministry from heaven conducted by the Christ of glory. His work was for him imbued with divine power, the lifeblood of the supernatural pulsed through it. His service, at each point where it touched men, marked the line and opened channels for the introduction of divine creative forces into human souls. So vivid was this consciousness of involvement in the supernatural, that nothing short of a comparison of God's word through him with the divine word at the first creation could adequately express it to Paul's mind: "God who said, Let light shine out of darkness, has shined into our hearts for the purpose of our imparting the light of the knowledge of his glory in the face of Jesus Christ." Nor was this close participation with God in a transforming spiritual process something glorious merely in itself. Paul also took into account its comprehensive effect. When the Apostle says "we all are transformed" it is evident that the statement is not limited to the Apostles or preachers of the Gospel, but includes, so far at least as the passive experience is concerned, all believers. To the joyous consciousness of exerting extraordinary power there was added the delight of witnessing extraordinary results. There is a note of genuine Christian universalism in this. It was a reason for profound satisfaction to Paul that he needed not stand in the midst of the congregation of God as another Moses, partaking of a light from God in which the others could not share, solitary in his splendor, but that the larger share of what he affirmed of himself had through him become the possession of the simplest believer, a transfiguration of spirit like his own by the beholding of the Lord. Refracted from numberless mirrors the light multiplied and intensified itself for each on whom it fell. Nevertheless even so a measure of incommunicable distinction remained. Since the reproduction into the likeness of Christ is dependent on and proportionate to the vision of the Savior, and since this vision from the nature of the case is more constantly present to the minister of the Gospel than to the common believer, it follows that in the former an altogether unique result may be expected. So it was undoubtedly with Paul. He had no need of testing the principle in others; a more direct and convincing evidence lay in its effect upon himself. He was aware of a renewal of the inner man, progressing from day to day, and in which there was observable this law of increase, that the more he did to make Christ known, the

deeper the lineaments of the character of Christ were
impressed upon his soul. Even the hardships befalling his
flesh in the service of the Lord were contributory to this:
"We are always bearing about in the body the dying of Jesus,
that the life also of Jesus may be manifested in our mortal
flesh." And: "Our light affliction, which is for the moment,
works for us more exceedingly an eternal weight of glory."
"Therefore we faint not, though our outward man decay,
yet the inner man is renewed day by day. "Thus the
Apostle's ministry, while exercised upon others, became
unto him an unintermittent ministry to his own soul, ever
increasingly assimilating him to the glory of Christ.

Such was Paul's conception of the ministry of the New
Covenant. It bears upon its face the marks of the historical
situation in which he was called upon to present it.
Nonetheless it has abiding validity, for it is drawn from the
nature of the Gospel itself, and the Gospel is the Gospel of
Him who remains the same yesterday and today and forever.
Even of the errors over against which Paul placed these
glorious views it is in a certain sense true that they are not of
one age but of all ages; they lead a life of pseudo-immortality
among men. In the Judaistic controversy which shook the
early church, forces and tendencies were at work deeply
rooted in the sinful human heart. In modernized apparel
they confront us still to the present day. There are still
abroad forms of a Christless Gospel. There prevails still a
subtle form of legalism which would rob the Savior of his
crown of glory, earned by the cross, and would make of
Him a second Moses, offering us the stones of the law

instead of the life bread of the Gospel. And, oh the pity and shame of it, the Jesus that is being preached but too often is a Christ after the flesh, a religious genius, the product of evolution, powerless to save! Let us pray that it may be given to the Church to repudiate and cast out this error with the resoluteness of Paul. There is need for her ministers of placing themselves ever afresh in the light of the great Apostolic consciousness revealed in our text. They should learn once more to bear their message out of the fulness of conviction that it is an unchangeable message, reliable as the veracity of God Himself. Grant God that it may become on the lips of his servants more truly from age to age a Gospel from which the name of Christ crowds out every other human name, good tidings of atonement and righteousness and supernatural renewal; to preacher and people alike, what it was to Paul and his converts, a mirror of vision and transfiguration after the image of the Lord.

VI. Heavenly-Mindedness

Hebrews 11:9–10:

"By faith he became a sojourner in the land of promise, as in a land not his own, dwelling in tents, with Isaac and Jacob, the heirs with him of the same promise; for he looked for the city which has the foundations, whose builder and maker is God"

The chapter from which our text is taken is preeminently
the chapter on faith. It Illustrates the nature, power and
effects of this grace in a series of examples from sacred
history. In the context the prophecy of Habakkuk is quoted:
"The righteous shall live by faith." We remember that in the
Epistle to the Romans and Galatians also the same prophecy
appears with prominence. Abraham likewise there figures as
the great example of faith. In consequence one might easily
be led to think that the development of the idea of faith in
these Epistles and in our chapter moves along identical lines.
This would be only partially correct. Although the two types
of teaching are in perfect accord, and touch each other at
certain points, yet the angle of vision is not the same. In
Romans and Galatians faith is in the main trust in the grace
of God, the instrument of justification, the channel through
which the vital influences flowing from Christ are received
by the believer. Here in Hebrews the conception is wider;
faith is "the proving of things not seen, the assurance of
things hoped for." It is the organ for apprehension of unseen
and future realities, giving access to and contact with
another world. It is the hand stretched out through the vast
distances of space and time, whereby the Christian draws to
himself the things far beyond, so that they become actual to
him. The earlier Epistles are not unfamiliar with this aspect
of faith. Paul in II Corinthians declares that for the present
the Christian walks through a land of faith and not of sight.
And on the other hand this chapter is not unfamiliar with the
justifying function of faith, for we are told of Noah, that he
became heir of the righteousness which is according to faith.

Nevertheless, taking the two representations as a whole, the distinctness of the point of view in each should not be neglected. It can be best appreciated by observing that, while in these other writings Christ is the object of faith, the One towards whom the sinner's trust is directed, here the Savior is described as Himself exercising faith, in fact as the one perfect, ideal believer. The writer exhorts his readers: "Let us run with patience the race that is set before us, looking unto Jesus the leader and perfecter of our faith." Faith in that other sense of specific trust, through which a guilty sinner becomes just in the sight of God, our Lord could not exercise, because He was sinless. But the faith that is an assurance of things hoped for and a proving of things not seen had a large place in his experience. By very reason of the contrast between the higher world to which He belonged and this dark lower world of suffering and death to which He had surrendered Himself it could not be otherwise than that faith, as a projection of his soul into the unseen and future, should have been the fundamental habit of the earthly life of his human nature, and should have developed in Him a degree of intensity not attained elsewhere. But, although, for the reason stated, in the unique case of Jesus the two types of faith did not go together, they by no means exclude each other in the mind of the Christian. For, after all, justifying faith is but a special application in one particular direction of the frame of mind here described. Among all the realities of the invisible world, mediated to us by the disclosures and promises of God, and to which our faith responds, there is none that more strongly calls into

action this faculty for grasping the unseen than the divine
pronouncement through the Gospel, that, though sinners,
we are righteous in the judgment of God. That is not only
the invisible, it seems the impossible; it is the paradox of all
paradoxes; it requires a unique energy of believing; it is the
supreme victory of faith over the apparent reality of things;
it credits God with calling the things that are not as though
they were; it penetrates more deeply into the deity of God
than any other act of faith.

What we read in this chapter about the various activities
and acts of faith in the lives of the Old Testament saints
might perhaps at first create the impression, that the word
faith is used in a looser sense, and that many things are
attributed to it not strictly belonging there on the author's
own definition. One might be inclined in more precise
language to classify them with other Christian graces. There
is certainly large variety of costume in the procession that is
made to pass before our eyes. The understanding that the
worlds were framed out of nothing, the ability to offer God
an acceptable sacrifice, the experience of translation unto
God, the preparing of the ark, the responsiveness to the call
to leave one's country, the power to conceive seed when
past age, the willingness to sacrifice an only son, Joseph's
making mention beforehand of the deliverance from Egypt,
and his giving commandment concerning his bones, the
hiding of the child Moses, the choice by Moses, when grown
up, of the reproach of God's people in preference to the
treasures of Egypt, all this and more is represented as
belonging to the one rubric of faith. But let us not

misunderstand the writer. When he affirms that by faith all these things were suffered and done, his idea is not that what is enumerated was in each case the direct expression of faith. What he means is that in the last analysis faith alone made possible every one of the acts described, that as an underlying frame of mind it enabled all these other graces to function, and to produce the rich fruitage here set forth. The obedience, the self-sacrifice, the patience, the fortitude, of all these the exercise in the profound Christian sense would have been impossible, if the saints had not had through faith their eye firmly fixed on the unseen and promised world. Whether the call was to believe or to follow, to do or to bear, the obedience to it sprang not from any earth fed sources but from the infinite reservoir of strength stored up in the mountain land above. If Moses endured it was not due to the power of resistance in his human frame, but because the weakness in him was compensated by the vision of Him who is invisible. If Abraham, who had gladly received the promises, offered up his only-begotten son, it was not because in heroic resignation he steeled himself to obedience, but because through faith he saw God as greater and stronger than the most inexorable physical law of nature: "For he accounted that God is able to raise up even from the dead." And so in all the other instances. Through faith the powers of the higher world were placed at the disposal of those whom this world threatened to overwhelm, and so the miracle resulted that from weakness they were made strong. No mistake could be greater than to naturalize the contents of this chapter, and to conceive of the thing portrayed as some instinct of idealism, some sort of sixth sense for what lies above the common plane of life, as people speak of men of vision, who see farther than the mass. The entire description rests on the basis of supernaturalism; these are annals of grace, magnalia Christi. Even the most illustrious names in the history of worldly achievement are not, as such, entitled to a place among them. This is the goodly company of patriarchs and prophets and saints, who endured the reproach of Christ, of whom the world was not worthy, who form the line of succession through which the promises passed, who now compose the cloud of witnesses that encompass our mortal strife, men of whom God is not ashamed to be called their God, with whom the Savior Himself is associated as the leader and finisher of the same faith.

In our text, however, we meet faith in its more simple and direct mode of operation. It appears as dealing with the unseen and future. From the life of the patriarchs the more militant, strenuous features are absent. In their lives it is allowed as in a region of seclusion and quietness to unfold before our eyes its simple beauty. Faith is here but another name for other worldliness or heavenly-mindedness. Herein lies the reason why the writer dwells with such evident delight upon this particular part of the Old Testament narrative. The other figures he merely sketches, and with a rapid skillful stroke of the brush puts in the highlights of their lives where the glory of faith illumined them. But the figure of Abraham he paints with the lingering, caressing hand of love, so that something of the serenity and peacefulness of the original patriarchal story is reproduced in the picture: "By faith he became a sojourner in the land of promise, as in a land not his own, dwelling in tents with Isaac and Jacob, the heirs with him of the same promise, for he looked for the city which has the foundations, whose builder and maker is God." The charm spread over this part of the subject to the author's vision also appears in this, that, after having already dismissed it and passed on to the portrayal of Abraham's faith in another form, as connected with the seed of the promise, he involuntarily returns to cast one more loving glance at it: "They died in faith, not having received the promises, but seen them and greeted them from afar, and having confessed that they were strangers and pilgrims on the earth. For they that say such things make it manifest that they are seeking after a country of their own. And if indeed they had been mindful of the country from which they went out, they would have had opportunity to return. But now they desire a better country, that is heavenly; wherefore God is not ashamed to be called their God: for He hath prepared them a city."

The other-worldliness of the patriarchs showed itself in this, that they confessed to be strangers and pilgrims on the earth. It found its visible expression in their dwelling in tents. Not strangers and pilgrims outside of Canaan, but strangers and pilgrims in the earth. The writer places all the emphasis on this, that they pursued their tent life in the very land of promise, which was their own, as in a land not their own. Only in this way is a clear connection between the staying in tents and the looking forward to heaven obtained.

For otherwise the tents might have signified merely that they considered themselves not at home when away from the holy land. If even in Canaan they carried within themselves the consciousness of pilgrimage then it becomes strikingly evident that it was a question of fundamental, comprehensive choice between earth and heaven. The adherence to the tent-life in the sight and amidst the scenes of the promised land fixes the aspiration of the patriarchs as aiming at the highest conceivable heavenly goal. It has in it somewhat of the scorn of the relative and of compromise. He who knows that for him a palace is in building does not dally with desires for improvement on a lower scale. Contentment with the lowest becomes in such a case profession of the highest, a badge of spiritual aristocracy with its proud insistence upon the ideal. Only the predestined inhabitants of the eternal city know how to conduct themselves in a simple tent as kings and princes of God.

As to its negative side, the feeling of strangeness on earth, even in Canaan, the writer could base his representation on the statement of Abraham to the sons of Heth: "I am a stranger and a sojourner with you," and on the words of the aged Jacob to Pharaoh: "The days of the years of my pilgrimage are an hundred and thirty years: few and evil have the days of the years of my life been, and have not attained unto the days of the years of the life of my fathers in the days of their pilgrimage." As to the positive side, the desire for a heavenly state, there is no such explicit testimony in the narrative of Genesis. Nonetheless the

author was fully justified in affirming this also. It is contained
by implication in the other. The refusal to build an abiding
habitation in a certain place must be due to the recognition
that one's true, permanent abode is elsewhere. The not-
feeling-at-home in one country has for its inevitable
counterpart homesickness for another. The writer plainly
ascribes this to the patriarchs, and in doing so also ascribes to
them a degree of acquaintance with the idea of a heavenly
life. His meaning is not that, unknown to themselves, they
symbolized through their mode of living the principle of
destination for heaven. On the contrary, we are expressly
told that they confessed, that they made it manifest, that
they looked for, that they desired. There existed with them
an intelligent and outspoken apprehension of the celestial
world. Let us not say that such an interpretation of their
minds is unhistorical, because they could not in that age have
possessed a clear knowledge of the world to come. Rather,
in reading this chapter on faith let us have faith, a large,
generous faith in the uniqueness and spiritual distinction of
the patriarchs as confessors, perhaps in advance of their
time, of the heaven-centered life of the people of God. In
other respects also Scripture represents the patriarchal
period as lifted above the average level of the surrounding
ages, even within the sphere of Special Revelation. Paul tells
us that in the matter of grace and freedom from the law
Abraham lived on a plane and in an atmosphere much higher
than that of subsequent generations. Anachronisms these
things are, if you will, but anachronisms of God, who does
not let Himself be bound by time, but, seeing the end from

the beginning, reserves the right to divide the flood of history, and to place on conspicuous islands at successive points great luminaries of his truth and grace shining far out into the future. The patriarchs had their vision of the heavenly country, a vision in the light of which the excellence or desirableness of every earthly home and country paled. Acquaintance with a fairer Canaan had stolen from their hearts the love of the land that lay spread around like a garden of paradise.

Of course, it does not necessarily follow from this that the author credits the patriarchs with a detailed, concrete knowledge of the heavenly world. In point of heavenly-mindedness he holds them up as models to be imitated. In point of information about the content of the celestial life he places the readers far above the reach of the Old Testament at its highest. To the saints of the New Covenant life and immortality and all the powers of the world to come have been opened up by Christ. The Christian state is as truly part and prelibation of the things above as a portal forms part of the house. If not wholly within, we certainly are come to Mount Zion, the city of the living God. And in this we are more than Abraham. No such Gospel broke in upon the solitude of these ancient shepherds, not even upon Jacob, when he saw the ladder reaching up into heaven with the angels of God ascending and descending upon it. But do you not see, that precisely on account of this difference in knowledge the faculty of faith had addressed to it a stronger challenge than it has in us, who pilgrim with heaven's door wide open in our sight? For this reason it is so profitable to return again and again to this part of the Old Testament Scriptures, and learn what great faith could do with less privilege, how precisely because it had such limited resource of knowledge, it made a sublimer flight, soaring with supreme dominion up to the highest heights of God.

Let us try briefly to analyze what this other-worldliness of the patriarchs involved, and in what respects it will be well for us to cultivate it. The first feature to be noted is that it is not essentially negative but positive in character. The core lies not in what it relinquishes but in what it seeks. Escape from the world here below and avoidance of the evil in the world do not furnish its primary motive. That is true only of the abnormal, morbid type of other-worldliness, that connected with pessimism and monastic seclusion. From an unwarranted identification with these the true grace portrayed by Scripture has been exposed to much ill-considered criticism and fallen into disrepute. If heavenly-mindedness were an upward flight in the ignominious sense of the word, it would be the very opposite to the heroism of genuine faith, a seeking for a harbor of refuge, instead of a steering for the haven of home. Do not misunderstand me. It is only right that in some measure the bitter experience of sin and evil should contribute to the Christian's desire for heaven. The attraction of heaven is in part the attraction of freedom from sin. And not a little of the contempt poured upon it, while pretending to protest against cloistered withdrawal, springs in reality from a defective perception of the seriousness of sin. Where the eye has not by divine grace been opened to the world's wickedness, it is easy to look with disdain on the Christian's world-shyness. But the Christian, who knows that the end of sin cannot come until the end of this world, looks at the question in a light of his own. He is fully warranted in considering ridicule of this kind part of the reproach of Christ and bearing it with joy. Nor should we forget, that an excess of interest in the present life, when shown in the name of religion, is apt, in our day, to be a symptom of doubt or unbelief in regard to the life to come. Still the principle remains in force, that the desirability of heaven should never possess exclusively or mainly negative significance. It is not something first brought into the religious mind through sin. The lineage and birth right of other-worldliness are of the oldest and noblest. By God Himself this traveler's unrest was implanted in the soul. Ever since the goal set by the Covenant of Works came within his ken, man carries with him in all his converse with this world the sense of appurtenance to another. This is but to say that supernaturalism forms from the outset the basis of true religion in man. Man belongs to two spheres. And Scripture not only teaches that these two spheres are distinct, it also teaches what estimate of relative importance ought to be placed upon them. Heaven is the primordial, earth the secondary creation. In heaven are the supreme realities; what surrounds us here below is a copy and shadow of the celestial things. Because the relation between the two spheres is positive, and not negative, not mutually repulsive, heavenly-mindedness can never give rise to neglect of the duties pertaining to the present life. It is the ordinance and will of God, that not apart from, but on the basis of, and in contact with, the earthly sphere man shall work out his heavenly destiny. Still the lower may never supplant the higher in our affections. In the heart of man time calls for eternity, earth for heaven. He must, if normal, seek the things above, as the flower's face is attracted by the sun, and the water courses are drawn to the ocean. Heavenly-mindedness, so far from blunting or killing the natural desires, produces in the believer a finer organization, with more delicate sensibilities, larger capacities, a stronger pulse of life. It does not spell impoverishment, but enrichment of nature. The spirit of the entire Epistle shows this. The use of the words "city" and "country" is evidence of it. These are terms that stand for the accumulation, the efflorescence, the intensive enjoyment of values. Nor should we overlook the social note in the representation. A perfect communion in a perfect society is promised. In the city of the living God believers are joined to the general assembly and church of the first born, and mingle with the spirits of just men made perfect. And all this faith recognizes. It does not first need the storms and stress that invade to quicken its desire for such things. Being the sum and substance of all the positive gifts of God to us in their highest form, heaven is of itself able to evoke in our hearts positive love, such absorbing love as can render us at times forgetful of the earthly strife. In such moments the transcendent beauty of the other shore and the irresistible current of our deepest life lift us above every regard of wind or wave. We know that through weather fair or foul our ship is bound straight for its eternal port. Next to the positiveness of its object the high degree of actuality in the working of this grace should be considered. Through the faith of heavenly-mindedness the things above reveal themselves to the believer, are present with him, and communicate themselves to him. Though as yet a pilgrim, the Christian is never wholly separated from the land of promise. His tents are pitched in close view of the city of God. Heaven is present to the believer's experience in no less real a sense than Canaan with its fair hills and valleys lay close to the vision of Abraham. He walks in the light of the heavenly world and is made acquainted with the kindred spirits inhabiting it. And since the word "actual" in its literal sense means "that which works," the life above possesses for the believer the highest kind of actuality. He is given to taste the powers of the world to come, as Abraham breathed the air of Canaan, and was refreshed by the dews descending on its fields. The roots of the Christian's life are fed from those rich and perennial springs that lie deep in the recesses of converse with God, where prayers ascend and divine graces descend, so that after each season of tryst he issues, a new man, from the secrecy of his tent. Because it had this effect for the patriarch's, faith had so intimately joined to it the exercise of hope. It is no less the assurance of things hoped for than the proving of things not seen. It annihilates the distance of time as much as of space. If faith deals with heaven as it exists, hope seizes upon it as it will be at the end. Hope attaches itself to promises; it sees and greets from afar. As the Epistle describes it, it does not contemplate purely provisional and earthly developments, does not come to rest in the happenings of intermediate ages, but relates to the end. In one unbroken flight it soars to the goal of God's work in history, which is none other than the finished heaven. For heaven itself is subject to a process of preparation, so that its full content became accessible only to the patriarchs through a projection of their faith in time. The heaven for which they hoped was the heaven of redemption, enriched through the ages, become peopled with the successive generations of the saints of God, filled with the glory of Christ, the recreated paradise, towards which all the streams of grace springing up in time send their waters. The believer requires this new heaven, not simply the cosmical place that resulted from the first creation. Hence his heavenly-mindedness can never destroy interest in the unfolding of the ways of God throughout the history of the present world. Neither grows he impatient when the promise seems to tarry. For his hope also is in him a vitalizing power. It lives by the things that are not as though they were already, and makes the future supply strength for the present. Amidst all the vicissitudes of time the Christian knows that the foundations of the city of God are being quietly laid, that its walls are rising steadily, and that it will at last stand finished in all its golden glory, the crowning product of the work of God for his own.

But the faith of heavenly-mindedness in yet another, even profounder, sense surmounts time. In contrast with what is transitory it lays hold of the unchanging and eternal. The text expresses this by describing the city looked for as the city which has the foundations. The difference between the well founded enduring edifice and the frail, collapsible tent has induced this turn of the figure. Already in the prophet Isaiah Jehovah declares: "Behold I lay in Zion for a foundation a stone, a precious corner-stone of sure foundation: he that believeth shall not make haste." In this word the two ideas of sure foundation and faith are brought into close connection. Because the foundation is sure the believer can lay aside all disquietude and impatience in regard to the working out of the divine purpose. He need not make haste. It is of the essence of faith to crave assurance; hence it cannot come to rest until it have cast its anchor into the eternal. And heaven above all else partakes of the character of eternity. It is the realm of the unchangeable. In this lower world time with its law of attrition is king. Nothing can escape his inexorable rule. What is must cease to be, what appears must vanish, what is built must be broken down, even though human heart should cherish it more than its own life. And this applies not merely to objects of natural affection; it involves also much that is of transitory purpose in the service and Church of God. Even our religion in its earthly exercise is not exempt from the tragical aspect borne by all existence in time. The summons comes again and again: "Get thee out of thy country, and: from thy kindred, and from thy father's house," and after a brief spell of comfort and delight we anew find ourselves in tents roaming through an inhospitable world. There is no help for these things. Like Abraham we must resolutely confess, that we are strangers and pilgrims in a land of time, and that the best this land can offer us is but a caravanserai to tarry in for a day and a night. Abraham would have undoubtedly rejoiced in the vision of the historical Jerusalem around which gather so many glories of God's redemptive work. But, suppose it had risen up before him in all its beauty, would that have been the soul satisfying vision his faith desired? No, there is neither quietness nor repose for the believer's heart except on the bosom of eternity. There and there alone is shelter from the relentless pursuit of change. The inspired writer tells us that the two most momentous events in sacred history, the giving of the law on Sinai and the end of the world, signify the removal of things that are shaken, in order that such things as are not shakable may remain. And the second shaking is so radical and comprehensive that it involves not only the earth but likewise the heavens: it will sweep the transitory out of the life of the people of God even in the higher regions, and will leave them, when the smoke and dust of the upheaval are blown away, in a clear atmosphere of eternal life. But in this sense also faith is not purely prospective it enables to anticipate; it draws down the imperishable substance of eternity into its vessel of time and feeds on it. The believer knows that even now there is in him that which has been freed from the law of change, a treasure that moth and rust cannot corrupt, true riches enshrined in his heart as in a treasury of God. Have we ever been impressed in reading the narrative of Genesis by the peacefulness and serenity enveloping the figures of the patriarchs? There is something else here besides the idyllic charm of rural surroundings. What enviable freedom from the unrest, the impatience, the feverish excitement of the children of this world! Our modern Christian life so often lacks the poise and stability of the eternal. Religion has come so overmuch to occupy itself with the things of time that it catches the spirit of time. Its purposes turn fickle and unsteady; its methods become superficial and ephemeral; it alters its course so constantly; it borrows so readily from sources beneath itself, that it undermines its own prestige in matters pertaining to the eternal world. Where lies the remedy? It would be useless to seek it in withdrawal from the struggles of this present world. The true corrective lies in this, that we must learn again to carry a heaven-fed and heaven-centered spirit into our walk and work below. The grand teaching of the Epistle that through Christ and the New Covenant the heavenly projects into the earthly, as the headlands of a continent project into the ocean, should be made fruitful for the whole tone and temper of our Christian service. Every task should be at the same time a means of grace from and an incentive to work for heaven. There has been One greater than Abraham, who lived his life in absolute harmony with this principle, in whom the fullest absorption in his earthly calling could not for a moment disturb the consciousness of being a child of heaven. Though, like unto the patriarchs. He had no permanent home, not even a tent, this was not in his case the result of a break with an earthly-minded past. It was natural to Him. In his mind were perfectly united the two hemispheres of supernaturalism, that of the source of power back of, and that of the eternal goal of life beyond every work. A religion that has ceased to set its face towards the celestial city, is bound sooner or later to discard also all supernatural resources in its endeavor to transform this present world. The days are perhaps not far distant when we shall find ourselves confronted with a quasi-form of Christianity professing openly to place its dependence on and to work for the present life alone, a religion, to use the language of Hebrews, become profane and a fornicator like Esau, selling for a mess of earthly pottage its heavenly birthright.

There are two more aspects of the patriarchal faith of heavenly-mindedness to be briefly considered. The first is its spirituality. Heavenly-mindedness is spiritual-mindedness. This pervades like an atmosphere the entire Epistle. We have already seen that even in the promised land the patriarchs remained tent-dwellers. God had a wise purpose in thus postponing for them personally the fulfilment of the temporal promise. Although Canaan was a goodly land, it was yet, after all, material and not of that higher substance we call spiritual. While capable of carrying up the mind to supernal regions, it also exposed to the danger of becoming satisfied with the blessing in its provisional form. That this danger was not imaginary the later history of Israel testifies. In order to guard against such a result in the case of the patriarchs God withheld from them the land and its riches and made of this denial a powerful spiritualizing discipline. By it they were led to reflect that, since the promise was theirs beyond all doubt, and yet they were not allowed to inherit it in its material form, that therefore it must in the last analysis relate to something far higher and different, something of which the visible and sensual is a mere image.

Thus the conception of another sphere of being was introduced into their minds: henceforth they sought the better country. Not as if the things of sense were worthless in themselves, but because they knew of something transcendent that claimed their supreme affection. Their tastes and enjoyments had been raised to another plane. The refinement of grace had been imparted to them. For bodily hands there had been, as it were, substituted spiritual antennae, sensitive to intangible things. They had come to a mountain that could not be touched and yet could be felt. In all the treasures and promises of religion the one valuable thing is this spiritual core. In the word that God speaks we can taste all his goodness and grace. Hope itself is spiritualized, remaining no longer the hope of imagination but grasping in God the ideal root from which the whole future must spring and blossom in due time. The heavenly world does not appear desirable as simply a second improved edition of this life; that would be nothing else than earthly-mindedness projected into the future. The very opposite takes place: heaven spiritualized in advance our present walk with God. Each time faith soars and alights behind the veil it brings back on its wings some of the subtle fragrance that there prevails. This also is an important principle in need of stress at the present day. If there is danger of Christianity being temporalized, there is no less danger of its being materialized. How easily do we fall into the habit of handling the things of our holy faith after an external, quantitative, statistical fashion, so that they turn flesh under our touch and emit a savor of earth? If at any time or in any form this fault should threaten to befall us, let us revisit the tents of the patriarchs and rehearse the lesson, that in religion the body without the soul is worthless and without power.

The other point to be observed is this, that heaven is the normal goal of our redemption. We all know that religion is older than redemption. At the same time the experience of redemption is the summit of religion. The two have become so interwoven that the Christian cannot conceive of a future state from which the redemptive mould and color would be absent. The deepest and dearest in us is so much the product of salvation, that the vision of God as such and the vision of God our Savior melt into one. We could not separate them if we would. The simple reason is that precisely in redeeming us God has revealed to us the inmost essence of his deity. No one but are deemed creature can truly know what it is for God to be God, and what it means to worship and possess Him as God. This is the fine gold of the Christian's experience, sweeter to him than honey and the honeycomb. The river that makes glad the city of God is the river of grace. The believer's mind and heart will only in heaven compass the full riches, the length and breadth and depth and height of the love of God. No one can drink so deeply of it here, but he will more deeply drink hereafter. Blessed be God, no stream of Lethe flows this side of his city to wash away from our minds the remembrance of redeeming grace! The life above will be a ceaseless coming to Jesus, the Mediator of a better covenant, and to the blood of sprinkling that speaketh better than Abel. The Lamb slain for ours sins will be all the glory of Emmanuel's land.

Finally the highest thing that can be spoken about this city is that it is the city of our God, that He is in the midst of it. Traced to its ultimate root heavenly-mindedness is the thirst of the soul after God, the living God. The patriarchs looked not for some city in general, but for a city whose builder and maker was God. It is characteristic of faith that it not merely desires the perfect but desires the perfect as a work and gift of God. A heaven that was not illumined by the light of God, and not a place for closest embrace of Him, would be less than heaven. God as builder and maker thereof has put the better part of Himself into his work. Therefore those who enter the city are in God. The thought is none other than that of the seer in the Apocalypse: "I saw no temple therein: for the Lord God, the Almighty and the Lamb are the temple thereof. And that city has no need of the sun, neither of the moon to shine upon it, for the glory of God lightens it, and the throne of God and the Lamb are therein: and his servants shall do Him service, and they shall see his face, and his name shall be on their foreheads." And the faith is the faith of the Psalmist, who spoke: "Whom have I in heaven but Thee, and there is none upon earth that I desire beside Thee." Here it is impossible for us to tell how truly and to what extent our relation to God is a relation of pure, disinterested love in which we seek Him for his own sake. There, when all want and sin frailty shall have slipped away from us, we shall be able to tell. It was because God discerned in the souls of the patriarchs, underneath all else, this personal love, this homesickness for Himself, that He caused to be recorded about them the greatest thing that can be spoken of any man: that God is not ashamed to be called their God, and that He has prepared for them the city of their desire.

THE IDEA OF BIBLICAL THEOLOGY AS A SCIENCE AND AS A THEOLOGICAL DISCIPLINE

INAUGURAL ADDRESS AT PRINCETON THEOLOGICAL SEMINARY

Tuesday, May 8th, 1894 at 12 o'clock

First Presbyterian Church, Princeton, NJ

by

THE REV. GEERHARDUS VOS, Ph.D., D.D.

PREFATORY NOTE

The Rev. Geerhardus Vos, Ph.D., D.D., was elected
Professor of Biblical Theology in Princeton Theological
Seminary at the spring meeting of the Board of Directors,
1893, and assumed the duties of the chair provisionally from
September, 1893. His formal induction into the chair took
place on Tuesday, May 8, 1894, at 12 o'clock, in the First
Presbyterian Church of Princeton.

Mr. President and Gentlemen of the Board of Directors:

It is with no little hesitation that I enter upon the work to which you have called me and to-day more formally introduced me. In reaching the conclusion that it was my duty to accept the call with which you had honored me, I was keenly alive to the incongruity of my name being associated in the remotest manner with the names of those illustrious men through whom God has glorified Himself in this institution. Some of those at whose feet I used to sit while a student here, are fallen asleep; a smaller number remain until now. The memory of the former as well as the presence of the latter make me realize my weakness even more profoundly than the inherent difficulty of the duties I shall have to discharge. While, however, on the one hand, there is something in these associations that might well fill me with misgivings at this moment, I shall not endeavor to conceal that on the other hand they are to me a source of inspiration. In view of my own insufficiency I rejoice all the more in having behind and around me this cloud of witnesses. I am thoroughly convinced that in no other place or environment could the sacred influences of the past be brought to bear upon me with a purer and mightier impulse to strengthen and inspire me than here. The pledge to which I have just subscribed is itself a symbol of this continuity between the past and the future; and I feel that it will act upon me, not merely by outward restraint, but with an inwardly constraining power, being a privilege as well as an obligation.

Although not a new study, yet Biblical Theology is a new chair, in this Seminary; and this fact has determined the choice of the subject on which I purpose to address you. Under ordinary circumstances, the treatment of some special subject of investigation would have been more appropriate, and perhaps more interesting to you, than a discussion of general principles. But Biblical Theology being a recent arrival in the Seminary curriculum and having been entrusted to my special care and keeping, I consider it my duty to introduce to you this branch of theological science, and to describe, in general terms at least, its nature and the manner in which I hope to teach it.

This is all the more necessary because of the wide divergence of opinion in various quarters concerning the standing of this newest accession to the circle of sacred studies. Some have lauded her to the skies as the ideal of scientific theology, in such extravagant terms as to reflect seriously upon the character of her sisters of greater age and longer standing. Others look upon the new-comer with suspicion, or even openly dispute her right to a place in the theological family. We certainly owe it to her and to ourselves to form a well-grounded and intelligent judgment on this question. I hope that what I shall say will in some degree shed light on the points at issue, and enable you to judge impartially and in accordance with the facts of the case.

Every discussion of what is to be understood by Biblical Theology ought to proceed from a clear understanding of what Theology is in general. Etymology, in many cases a safer guide than *a priori* constructions, tells us that Theology is *knowledge concerning God*, and this primitive definition is fully supported by encyclopædic principles. Only when making Theology knowledge concerning God do we have the right to call it a separate science. Sciences are not formed at haphazard, but according to an objective principle of division. As in general science is bound by its object and must let itself be shaped by reality; so likewise the classification of sciences, the relation of the various members in the body of universal knowledge, has to follow the great lines by which God has mapped out the immense field of the universe. The title of a certain amount of knowledge to be called a separate science depends on its reference to such a separate and specific object as is marked off by these God-drawn lines of distinction. We speak of a science of Biology, because God has made the phenomena of life distinct from those of inorganic being. Now, from this point of view we must say that no science has a clearer title to separate existence than Theology. Between God as the Creator and all other things as created the distinction is absolute. There is not another such gulf within the universe. God, as distinct from the creature, is the only legitimate object of Theology.

It will be seen, however, on a moment's reflection, that Theology is not merely distinguished from the other sciences by its object, but that it also sustains an altogether unique relation to this object, for which no strict analogy can be found elsewhere. In all the other sciences man is the one who of himself takes the first step in approaching the objective world, in subjecting it to his scrutiny, in compelling it to submit to his experiments—in a word, man is the one who proceeds actively to make nature reveal her facts and her laws. In Theology this relation between the subject and object is reversed. Here it is God who takes the first step to approach man for the purpose of disclosing His nature, nay, who creates man in order that He may have a finite mind able to receive the knowledge of His infinite perfections. In Theology the object, far from being passive, by the act of creation first posits the subject over against itself, and then as the living God proceeds to impart to this subject that to which of itself it would have no access. For "the things of God none knoweth, save the Spirit of God." Strictly speaking, therefore, we should say that not God in and for Himself, but God in so far as He has revealed Himself, is the object of Theology.

Though applying to Theology in the abstract and under all circumstances, this unique character has been emphasized by the entrance of sin into the human race. In his sinful condition, while retaining some knowledge of God, man for all pure and adequate information in divine things is absolutely dependent on that new self-disclosure of God which we call supernatural revelation. By the new birth and the illumination of the mind darkened through sin, a new subject is created. By the objective self-manifestation of God as the Redeemer, a new order of things is called into being. And by the depositing of the truth concerning this new order of things in the Holy Scriptures, the human mind is enabled to obtain that new knowledge which is but the reflection in the regenerate consciousness of an objective world of divine acts and words.

This being so, it follows immediately that the beginning of all our Theology consists in the appropriation of that supernatural process by which God has made Himself the object of our knowledge. We are not left to our own choice here, as to where we shall begin our theological study. The very nature of Theology requires us to begin with those branches which relate to the revelation-basis of our science. Our attitude from the outset must be a dependent and receptive one. To let the image of God's self-revelation in the Scriptures mirror itself as fully and clearly as possible in his mind, is the first and most important duty of every theologian. And it is in accordance with this principle that, in the development of scientific theology through the ages, a group of studies have gradually been separated from the rest and begun to form a smaller organism among themselves, inasmuch as the receptive attitude of the theological consciousness toward the source of revelation was the common idea underlying and controlling them. This group is usually designated by the name of Exegetical Theology. Its formation was not a matter of mere accident, nor the result of definite agreement among theologians; the immanent law of the development of the science, as rooted in its origin, has brought it about in a natural manner.

In classifications of this kind general terms are apt to acquire more or less indefinite meanings. They tend to become formulas used for the purpose of indicating that certain studies belong together from a practical point of view or according to a methodological principle. In many cases it would be fanciful to seek any other than a practical justification for grouping certain branches together. So it is clear on the surface that much is subsumed under the department of Exegetical Theology, which bears only a very remote and indirect relation to its central idea. There are subservient and preparatory studies lying in the periphery and but loosely connected with the organic centre. Nevertheless, if Exegetical Theology is to be more than a conglomerate of heterogeneous studies, having no other than a practical unity, we must expect that at its highest point of development it will appear to embody one of the necessary forms of the essential idea of all Theology, and will unfold itself as *knowledge concerning God* in the strict sense of the term. The science in which this actually happens will be the heart of the organism of Exegetical Theology.

Exegetical Theology deals with God under the aspect of Revealer of Himself and Author of the Scriptures. It is naturally divided into two parts, of which the one treats of the formation of the Scriptures, the other of the actual revelation of God lying back of this process. We further observe that the formation of the Scriptures serves no other purpose than to perpetuate and transmit the record of God's self-disclosure to the human race as a whole. Compared with revelation proper, the formation of the Scriptures appears as a means to an end. Bibliology with all its adjuncts, therefore, is not the centre of Exegetical Theology, but is logically subordinated to the other division, which treats of

revelation proper. Or, formulating it from the human point
of view, all our investigations as to the origin of the
Scriptures, their collection into a Canon, their original text,
as well as the exegetical researches by which the contents of
the Biblical writings are inductively ascertained, ultimately
serve the one purpose of teaching us what God has revealed
concerning Himself. None of these studies find their aim in
themselves, but all have their value determined and their
place assigned by the one central study to which they are
leading up and in which they find their culminating point.
This central study that gives most adequate and natural
expression to the idea of Exegetical Theology is Biblical
Theology.

In general, then, Biblical Theology is that part of
Exegetical Theology which deals with the revelation of God.
It makes use of all the results that have been obtained by all
the preceding studies in this department. Still, we must
endeavor to determine more precisely in what sense this
general definition is to be understood. For it might be said of
Systematic Theology, nay of the whole of Theology, with
equal truth, that it deals with supernatural revelation. The
specific character of Biblical Theology lies in this, that it
discusses both the form and contents of revelation from the
point of view of the revealing activity of God Himself. In
other words, it deals with revelation in the active sense, as
an act of God, and tries to understand and trace and describe
this act, so far as this is possible to man and does not elude
our finite observation. In Biblical Theology both the form
and contents of revelation are considered as parts and

products of a divine work. In Systematic Theology these
same contents of revelation appear, but not under the aspect
of the stages of a divine work; rather as the material for a
human work of classifying and systematizing according to
logical principles. Biblical Theology applies no other method
of grouping and arranging these contents than is given in the
divine economy of revelation itself.

From this it follows that, in order to obtain a more
definite conception of Biblical Theology, we must try to
gather the general features of God's revealing work. Here,
as in other cases, the organism of a science can be conceived
and described only by anticipating its results. The following
statements, accordingly, are not to be considered in the light
of an *a priori* construction, but simply formulate what the
study of Biblical Theology itself has taught us.

The first feature characteristic of supernatural revelation
is *its historical progress.* God has not communicated to us the
knowledge of the truth as it appears in the calm light of
eternity to his own timeless vision. He has not given it in the
form of abstract propositions logically correlated and
systematized. The simple fact that it is the task of Systematic
Theology to reproduce revealed truth in such form, shows
that it does not possess this form from the beginning. The
self-revelation of God is a work covering ages, proceeding in
a sequence of revealing words and acts, appearing in a long
perspective of time. The truth comes in the form of growing
truth, not truth at rest. No doubt the explanation of this fact
is partly to be sought in the finiteness of the human

understanding. Even that part of the knowledge of God
which has been revealed to us is so overwhelmingly great
and so far transcends our human capacities, is such a flood of
light, that it had, as it were, gradually to be let in upon us,
ray after ray, and not the full radiancy at once. By imparting
the elements of the knowledge of Himself in a divinely-
arranged sequence God has pointed out to us the way in
which we might gradually grasp and truly know Him. This
becomes still more evident, if we remember that this
revelation is intended for all ages and nations and classes and
conditions of men, and therefore must adapt itself to the
most various characters and temperaments by which it is to
be assimilated.

We feel, however, that this explanation, however
plausible in itself, is but a partial one, and can never
completely satisfy. The deeper ground for the historic
character of revelation cannot lie in the limitations of the
human subject, but must be sought in the nature of
revelation itself. Revelation is not an isolated act of God,
existing without connection with all the other divine acts of
supernatural character. It constitutes a part of that great
process of the new creation through which the present
universe as an organic whole shall be redeemed from the
consequences of sin and restored to its ideal state, which it
had originally in the intention of God. Now, this new
creation, in the objective, universal sense, is not something
completed by a single act all at once, but is a history with its
own law of organic development. It could not be otherwise,
inasmuch as at every point it proceeds on the basis of and in

contact with the natural development of this world and of the human race, and, the latter being in the form of history, the former must necessarily assume that form likewise. It is simply owing to our habit of unduly separating revelation from this comprehensive background of the total redeeming work of God, that we fail to appreciate its historic, progressive nature. We conceive of it as a series of communications of abstract truth forming a body by itself, and are at a loss to see why this truth should be parcelled out to man little by little and not given in its completeness at once. As soon as we realize that revelation is at almost every point interwoven with and conditioned by the redeeming activity of God in its wider sense, and together with the latter connected with the natural development of the present world, its historic character becomes perfectly intelligible and ceases to cause surprise.

In this great redeeming process two stages are to be distinguished. First come those acts of God which have a universal and objective significance, being aimed at the production of an organic centre for the new order of things. After this has been accomplished, there follows a second stage during which this objective redemption is subjectively applied to individuals. In both the stages the supernatural element is present, though in the former, owing to its objective character, it appears more distinctly than in the latter. The whole series of redeeming acts, culminating in the incarnation and atoning work of the Mediator and the pouring out of the Holy Spirit, bears the signature of the miraculous on its very face. But the supernatural, though not objectively controllable, is none the less present during the later stage in each case where an individual soul is regenerated. Revelation as such, however, is not coextensive with this whole process in both its stages. Its history is limited to the former half, that is, it accompanies in its progress the gradual unfolding of the central and objective salvation of God, and no sooner is the latter accomplished than revelation also has run its course and its voice ceases to speak. The reason for this is obvious. The revelation of God being not subjective and individual in its nature, but objective and addressed to the human race as a whole, it is but natural that this revelation should be embedded in the channels of the great objective history of redemption and extend no further than this. In point of fact, we see that, when the *finished* salvation worked out among Israel is stripped of its particularistic form to extend to all nations, at the same moment the *completed* oracles of God are given to the human race as a whole to be henceforth subjectively studied and appropriated. It is as unreasonable to expect revelations after the close of the Apostolic age as it would be to think that the great saving facts of that period can be indefinitely increased and repeated.

Even this, however, is not sufficient to show the historic character of revelation in its full extent. Up to this point we have only seen how the disclosure of truth in general follows the course of the history of redemption. We now must add that in not a few cases revelation is *identified* with history. Besides making use of words, God has also employed acts to reveal great principles of truth. It is not so much the prophetic visions or miracles in the narrower sense that we think of in this connection. We refer more specially to those great, supernatural, history-making acts of which we have examples in the redemption of the covenant-people from Egypt, or in the crucifixion and resurrection of Christ. In these cases the history itself forms a part of revelation. There is a self-disclosure of God in such acts. They would speak even if left to speak for themselves. Forming part of history, these revealing acts necessarily assume historical relations among themselves, and succeed one another according to a well-defined principle of historical sequence. Furthermore, we observe that this system of revelation-acts is not interpolated into the larger system of biblical history after a fanciful and mechanical fashion. The relation between the two systems is vital and organic. These miraculous interferences of God to which we ascribe a revealing character, furnish the great joints and ligaments by which the whole framework of sacred history is held together, and its entire structure determined. God's saving deeds mark the critical epochs of history, and as such, have continued to shape its course for centuries after their occurrence.

Of course we should never forget that, wherever revelation and the redemptive acts of God coincide, the latter frequently have an ulterior purpose extending beyond the sphere of revelation. The crucifixion and resurrection of Christ were acts not exclusively intended to reveal something to man, but primarily intended to serve some definite purpose in reference to God. Insofar as they satisfied the divine justice it would be inaccurate to view them under the aspect of revelation primarily or exclusively. Nevertheless, the revealing element is essential even in their case, the two ends of satisfaction and of revelation being combined into one. And in the second place, we must remember that the revealing acts of God never appear separated from His verbal communications of truth. Word and act always accompany each other, and in their interdependence strikingly illustrate our former statement, to the effect that revelation is organically connected with the introduction of a new order of things into this sinful world. Revelation is the light of this new world which God has called into being. The light needs the reality and the reality needs the light to produce the vision of the beautiful creation of His grace. To apply the Kantian phraseology to a higher subject, without God's acts the words would be empty, without His words the acts would be blind.

A second ground for the historic character of revelation may be found in its eminently practical aspect. The knowledge of God communicated by it is nowhere for a purely intellectual purpose. From beginning to end it is a knowledge intended to enter into the actual life of man, to be worked out by him in all its practical bearings. The Shemitic, and in particular the Biblical, conception of knowledge is distinguished from the Greek, more intellectualistic idea, by the prominence of this practical element. To know, in the Shemitic sense, is to have the consciousness of the reality and the properties of something interwoven with one's life through the closest intercourse and communion attainable. Now in this manner God has interwoven the supernaturally communicated knowledge of Himself with the historic life of the chosen race, so as to secure for it a practical form from the beginning. Revelation is connected throughout with the fate of Israel. Its disclosures arise from the necessities of that nation, and are adjusted to its capacities. It is such a living historical thing that it has shaped the very life of this nation into the midst of which it descended. The importance of this aspect of revelation has found its clearest expression in the idea of the covenant as the form of God's progressive self-communication to Israel. God has not revealed Himself in a school, but in the covenant; and the covenant as a communion of life is all-comprehensive, embracing all the conditions and interests of those contracting it. There is a knowledge and an imparting of knowledge here, but in a most practical way and not merely by theoretical instruction.

If in the foregoing we have correctly described the most general character of revelation, we may enlarge our definition of Biblical Theology by saying that it is that part of Exegetical Theology which deals with the revelation of God in its historic continuity. We must now advance beyond this and inquire more particularly in what specific type of history God has chosen to embody His revelation. The idea of historic development is not sufficiently definite of itself to explain the manner in which divine truth has been progressively revealed. It is not until we ascribe to this progress an organic character that the full significance of the historic principle springs into view.

The truth of revelation, if it is to retain its divine and absolute character at all, must be perfect from the beginning. Biblical Theology deals with it as a product of a supernatural divine activity, and is therefore bound by its own principle to maintain the perfection of revealed truth in all its stages. When, nevertheless, Biblical Theology also undertakes to show how the truth has been gradually set forth in greater fullness and clearness, these two facts can be reconciled in no other way than by assuming that the advance in revelation resembles the organic process, through which out of the perfect germ the perfect plant and flower and fruit are successively produced.

Although the knowledge of God has received material increase through the ages, this increase nowhere shows the features of external accretion, but throughout appears as an internal expansion, an organic unfolding from within. The elements of truth, far from being mechanically added one to the other in lifeless succession, are seen to grow out of each other, each richer and fuller disclosure of the knowledge of God having been prepared for by what preceded, and being in its turn preparatory for what follows. That this is actually so, follows from the soteriological purpose which revelation in the first instance is intended to serve. At all times, from the very first to the last, revealed truth has been kept in close contact with the wants and emergencies of the living generation. And these human needs, notwithstanding all variations of outward circumstance, being essentially the same in all periods, it follows that the heart of divine truth, that by which men live, must have been present from the outset, and that each subsequent increase consisted in the unfolding of what was germinally contained in the beginning of revelation. The Gospel of Paradise is such a germ in which the Gospel of Paul is potentially present; and the Gospel of Abraham, of Moses, of David, of Isaiah and Jeremiah, are all expansions of this original message of salvation, each pointing forward to the next stage of growth, and bringing the Gospel-idea one step nearer to its full realization. In this Gospel of Paradise we already discern the essential features of a covenant-relation, though the formal notion of a covenant does not attach to it. And in the covenant-promises given to Abraham these very features reappear, assume greater distinctness, and are seen to grow together, to crystallize as it were, into the formal covenant. From this time onward the expansive character of the covenant-idea shows itself. The covenant of Abraham contains the promise of the Sinaitic covenant; the latter again, from its very nature, gives rise to prophecy; and prophecy guards the covenant of Sinai from assuming a fixed, unalterable form, the prophetic word being a creative word under the influence of which the spiritual, universal germs of the covenant are quickened and a new, higher order of things is organically developed from the Mosaic theocracy, that new covenant of which Jeremiah spoke, and which our Saviour brought to light by the shedding of His blood. So dispensation grows out of dispensation, and the newest is but the fully expanded flower of the oldest.

The same principle may also be established more objectively, if we consider the specific manner in which God realizes the renewal of this sinful kosmos in accordance with His original purpose. This renewal is not brought about by mechanically changing one part after the other. God's method is much rather that of creating within the organism of the present world the centre of the world of redemption, and then organically building up the new order of things around this centre. Hence from the beginning all redeeming acts of God aim at the creation and introduction of this new organic principle, which is none other than Christ. All Old Testament redemption is but the saving activity of God working toward the realization of this goal, the great supernatural prelude to the Incarnation and the Atonement. And Christ having appeared as the head of the new humanity and having accomplished His atoning work, the further renewal of the kosmos is effected through an organic extension of His power in ever widening circles. In this sense the Apostle speaks of the fashioning anew of the body of our humiliation, that it may be conformed to the body of the glory of Christ, saying that this will happen *"according to the working whereby He is able to subject even all things unto Himself"* (Phil. 3:21). If, then, this supernatural process of transformation proceeds on organic principles, and if, as we have shown, revelation is but the light accompanying it in its course, the reflection of its divine realities in the sphere of knowledge, we cannot escape from the conclusion that revelation itself must exhibit a similar organic progress. In point of fact, we find that the actual working of Old Testament redemption toward the coming of Christ in the flesh, and the advance of revealed knowledge concerning

Christ, keep equal pace everywhere. The various stages in the gradual concentration of Messianic prophecy, as when the human nature of our Saviour is successively designated as the seed of the woman, the seed of Abraham, the seed of Judah, the seed of David, His figure assuming more distinct features at each narrowing of the circle—what are they but disclosures of the divine counsel corresponding in each case to new realities and new conditions created by His redeeming power? And as in the history of redemption there are critical stages in which the great acts of God as it were accumulate, so we find that at such junctures the process of revelation is correspondingly accelerated, and that a few years show, perhaps, more rapid growth and greater expansion than centuries that lie between. For, although the development of the root may be slow and the stem and leaves may grow almost imperceptibly, there comes a time when the bud emerges in a day and the flower expands in an hour to our wondering sight.* Such epochs of quickened revelation were the times of Abraham, of Moses, of David, and especially the days of the Son of Man.

This progress, moreover, increases in rapidity the nearer revelation approaches to its final goal. What rich developments, what wealth of blossoming and fruitage are compressed within the narrow limits of that period—no more than one lifetime—that is covered by the New Testament! In this, indeed, we have the most striking proof of the organic nature of the progress of revelation. Every organic development serves to embody an idea; and as soon as this idea has found full and adequate expression, the organism receives the stamp of perfection and develops no further. Because the New Testament times brought the final realization of the divine counsel of redemption as to its objective and central facts, therefore New Testament revelation brought the full-grown Word of God, in which the new-born world, which is complete in Christ, mirrors itself. In this final stage of revelation the deepest depths of eternity are opened up to the eye of Apostle and Seer. Hence, the frequent recurrence of the expression, "before the foundation of the world." We feel at every point that the last veil is drawn aside and that we stand face to face with the disclosure of the great mystery which was hidden in the divine purpose through the ages. All salvation, all truth in regard to man, has its eternal foundation in the Triune God Himself. It is this Triune God who here reveals Himself as the everlasting reality, from whom all truth proceeds, whom all truth reflects, be it the little streamlet of Paradise or the broad river of the New Testament losing itself again in the ocean of eternity. After this nothing higher can come. All the separate lines along which through the ages revelation was carried, have converged and met at a single point. The seed of the woman and the Angel of Jehovah are become one in the Incarnate Word. And as Christ is glorified once for all, so from the crowning glory and perfection of His revelation in the New Testament nothing can be taken away; nor can anything be added thereunto.

There is one more feature of the organic character of revelation which I must briefly allude to. Historic progress is not the only means used by God to disclose the full contents of His eternal Word. Side by side with it, we witness a striking multiformity of teaching employed for the same purpose. All along the historic stem of revelation, branches are seen to shoot forth, frequently more than one at a time, each of which helps to realize the complete idea of the truth for its own part and after its own peculiar manner. The legal, the prophetic, the poetic elements in the Old Testament are clearly-distinct types of revelation, and in the New Testament we have something corresponding to these in the Gospels, the Epistles, the Apocalypse. Further, within the limits of these great divisions there are numerous minor variations, closely associated with the peculiarities of individual character. Isaiah and Jeremiah are distinct, and so are John and Paul. And this differentiation rather increases than decreases with the progress of sacred history. It is greater in the New Testament than in the Old. The laying of the historic basis for Israel's covenant-life has been recorded by one author, Moses; the historic basis of the New Testament dispensation we know from the fourfold version of the Gospels. The remainder of the New Testament writings are in the form of letters, in which naturally the personal element predominates. The more fully the light shone upon the realization of the whole counsel of God and disclosed its wide extent, the more necessary it became to expound it in all its bearings, to view it at different angles, thus to bring out what Paul calls the *much-variegated*, the manifold, wisdom of God. For, God having chosen to reveal the truth through human instruments, it follows that these instruments must be both numerous and of varied adaptation to the common end. Individual coloring, therefore, and a peculiar manner of representation are not only not detrimental to a full statement of the truth, but directly subservient to it. God's method of revelation includes the very shaping and chiselling of individualities for His own objective ends. To put it concretely: we must not conceive of it as if God found Paul "ready-made," as it were, and in using Paul as an organ of revelation, had to put up with the fact that the dialectic mind of Paul reflected the truth in a dialectic, dogmatic form to the detriment of the truth. The facts are these: the truth having inherently, besides other aspects, a dialectic and dogmatic side, and God intending to give this side full expression, chose Paul from the womb, moulded his character, and gave him such a training that the truth revealed through him necessarily bore the dogmatic and dialectic impress of His mind. The divine objectivity and the human individuality here do not collide, nor exclude each other, because the man Paul, with his whole character, his gifts, and his training, is subsumed under the divine plan. The human is but the glass through which the divine light is reflected, and all the sides and angles into which the glass has been cut serve no other purpose than to distribute to us the truth in all the riches of its prismatic colors.

In some cases growth in the organism of revelation is closely dependent on this variety in the type of teaching. There are instances in which two or more forms of the one truth have been brought to light simultaneously, each of which exercised a deepening and enlarging influence upon the others. The Gospel of John contains revelations contemporaneous with those of the Synoptists, so that chronologically we can distribute its material over the pages of Matthew, Mark, and Luke. Nevertheless, taken as a whole and in its unity, the Gospel of John represents a fuller and wider self-revelation of Christ than the Synoptists; and not only so, but it also represents a type of revelation which presupposes the facts and teachings of the other Gospels, and is, in point of order, subsequent to them. The same thing might be said of Isaiah in its relation to Micah. So the variety itself contributes to the progress of revelation. Even in these cases of contemporaneous development along distinct lines and in independent directions, there is a mysterious force at work, which makes "the several parts grow out of and into each other with mutual support, so that the whole body is fitly joined together and compacted by that which every joint supplies, according to the effectual working in the measure of every part."

We may now perhaps attempt to frame a complete definition of our science. The preceding remarks have shown that the divine work of revelation did not proceed contrary to all law, but after a well-defined organic principle. Wherever there is a group of facts sufficiently distinct from their environment, and determined by some law of orderly sequence, we are justified in making these facts the object of scientific discussion. Far from there being in the conception of Biblical Theology anything at variance with the idea of Theology as based on the revealed knowledge of God, we have found that the latter even directly postulates the former. Biblical Theology, rightly defined, is nothing else than *the exhibition of the organic progress of supernatural revelation in its historic continuity and multiformity.*

It must be admitted, however, that not everything passing under the name of Biblical Theology satisfies the requirements of this definition. From the end of the preceding century, when our science first appears as distinct from Dogmatic Theology, until now, she has stood under the spell of un-Biblical principles. Her very birth took place under an evil star. It was the spirit of Rationalism which first led to distinguishing in the contents of the Scriptures between what was purely human, individual, local, temporal—in a word, conditioned by the subjectivity of the writers—and what was eternally valid, divine truth. The latter, of course, was identified with the teachings of the shallow Rationalism of that period. Thus Biblical Theology, which can only rest on the basis of revelation, began with a denial of this basis; and a science, whose task it is to set forth the historic principles of revelation, was trained up in a school notorious for its lack of historic sense. For to this type of Rationalism history, as such, is the realm of the contingent, the relative, the arbitrary, whilst only the deliverances of pure reason possess the predicate of absoluteness and universal validity. In this Biblical Theology of Rationalism, therefore, the historical principle merely served to eliminate or neutralize the revelation-principle. And since that time all the philosophical tendencies that have influenced Theology in general have also left their impress upon Biblical Theology in particular. It is not necessary for our present purpose to trace the various lines and currents of this complicated history; the less so since there can be no doubt but that they are rapidly merging into the great stream of Evolutionistic Philosophy, which, whatever truth there may be in its application to certain groups of phenomena, yet, as a general theory of the universe, is the most direct antithesis to the fundamental principles of revelation and Christianity.

That the influence of this philosophy, as it expresses and in turn moulds the spirit of the age, is perceptible in the field of Theology everywhere, no careful observer of recent events will deny. But Biblical Theology is, perhaps, more than any other branch of theological study affected by it, because its principle of historic progress in revelation seems to present certain analogies with the evolutionary scheme, and to offer exceptional opportunities for applying the latter, without departing too far from the real contents of Scripture. This analogy, of course, is merely formal, and from a material point of view there is a world-wide difference between that philosophy of history which the Bible itself outlines, and which alone Biblical Theology, if it wishes to remain Biblical, has a right to adopt, and, on the other hand, the so-called facts of the Bible pressed into the evolutionary formulas. It is especially in two respects that the principles of this philosophy have worked a radical departure from the right treatment of our science as it is prescribed by both the supernatural character of Christianity and the nature of Theology. In the first place, evolution is bent upon showing that the process of development is everywhere from the lower and imperfect to the higher and relatively more perfect forms, from impure beginnings through a gradual purification to some ideal end. So in regard to the knowledge of God, whose growth we observe in the Biblical writings, evolution cannot rest until it shall have traced its gradual advance from sensual, physical conceptions to ethical and spiritual ideas, from Animism and Polytheism to Monolatry and Monotheism. But this of necessity rules out the revelation-factor from Biblical Theology. Revelation as an act of God, theistically conceived of, can in no wise be associated with anything imperfect or impure or below the standard of absolute truth. However much Christian people may blind themselves to the fact, the outcome will show, as it does already show, that the principles of supernatural redemption and natural evolution are mutually exclusive. Hence, even now, those who accept the evolutionary construction of Biblical history, either openly and without reserve renounce the idea of supernatural revelation, or strip it of its objectivity so as to make it less antagonistic to that of natural development. In the same degree, however, that the latter is done, revelation loses its distinctively theistic character and begins to assume more and more the features of a Pantheistic process, that is, it ceases to be revelation in the commonly accepted sense of the term.

In the second place, the philosophy of evolution has corrupted Theology by introducing its leaven of metaphysical Agnosticism. Inasmuch as only the phenomenal world can become an object of knowledge to us and not the mysterious reality hidden behind the phenomena, and inasmuch as Theology in the old, traditional sense pretended to deal with such metaphysical realities as God and heaven and immortality, it follows that Theology must either be entirely abolished, or must submit to such a reconstruction as will enable her to retain a place among the phenomenalistic sciences. The former would be the more consistent and scientific, but the latter is usually preferred; because it is difficult at one stroke to set aside a thing so firmly rooted in the past. Theology, therefore, is now defined as *the science of religion*, and that, too, in the sense chiefly of a phenomenology of religion, in which by far the greater part of the investigation is devoted to the superficial external side of religion, and the heart of the matter receives scant treatment. Applied to Biblical Theology, this principle involves that no longer the historic progress of the supernatural revelation of God, but *the development of the religion* recorded in the Biblical writings, shall become the object of our science. Theology having become the science of religion, Biblical Theology must needs become the history of one, be it the greatest, of all religions, the history of the religion of Israel and of primitive Christianity.

How far this evil has penetrated may be inferred from the fact that there is scarcely a book on Biblical Theology in existence in which this conception of the object of our science is not met with, and in which it does not very largely determine the point of view. It has even vitiated so excellent a work in many respects as Oehler's Old Testament Theology. Of course, there are many degrees in the thoroughness with which this subjectivizing principle is carried through and applied. Between those who are just beginning to descend the ladder and those who have reached its lowest step, there is a very appreciable difference.

First, there are those who think that, though God has supernaturally revealed Himself in words and acts, nevertheless this revelation pure and simple, cannot be for us an object of scientific discussion, except in so far as it has blended with and produced its effect upon the religious consciousness of the people to whom it was given; and that, consequently, we must posit as the object of Biblical Theology the religion of the Bible, and can hope at the utmost to reason back from this religion as the result, to revelation as the cause that has produced it. To this we would answer, that there is no reason to make Biblical Theology, so conceived, a separate science. The investigation of the religion of Israel as a subjective phenomenon, together with the objective factors called in to explain it, belongs nowhere else than in the department of Biblical History. Furthermore, we believe that the Bible itself has recorded for us the interaction of the objective and the subjective factors in sacred history in such a manner that their joint product is nowhere made the central thought of its teaching, but much rather we are invited everywhere to fix our gaze on the objective self-revelation of God, and only in the second place to observe the subjective reflex of this divine activity in the religious consciousness of the people.

Others are more reserved in their recognition of the supernatural. They would confine the revelation of God to acts, and derive all the doctrinal contents of the Bible from the source of human reflection upon these divine acts. In this manner a compromise is obtained, whereby both the objectivity of revelation and the subjective development of Biblical teaching can be affirmed. This view is unsatisfactory, because it loses sight of the analogy between divine revelation and the ordinary way in which man communicates his thoughts. To man, made in the image of God, speech is the highest instrument of revealing Himself, and it would be strange if God in His self-disclosure entirely dispensed with the use of this instrument. Nor does this view leave any place for prophecy. The prophetic word is frequently a divine word preceding the divine act. Although, as we have seen, the progress of revelation is clearly conditioned by the actual realization of God's plan of redemption, yet this by no means implies that the saving deeds of God always necessarily go before, and the revelations which cast light on them always follow. In many cases the revealing word comes as an anticipation of the approaching events, as a flash of lightning preceding the thunder of God's judgments. As Amos strikingly expresses it: "Surely the Lord God will do nothing, but He revealeth His secret unto His servants the prophets" (3:7).

The supernatural factor, however, is reduced to still smaller proportions and entirely deprived of its objectivity by a third group of writers on Biblical Theology. According to these, supernatural revelation does not involve the communication of divine thoughts to man in any direct manner either by words or by actions. Revelation consists in this, that the Divine Spirit, by an unconscious process, stirs the depths of man's heart so as to cause the springing up therein afterward of certain religious thoughts and feelings, which are as truly human as they are a revelation of God, and are, therefore, only relatively true. It is owing to the influence of the Ritschlian or Neo-Kantian school of Theology that this view has gained new prevalence of late. The people of Israel are held to have possessed a creative religious genius, just as the Greek nation was endowed with a creative genius in the sphere of art. And, although the productions of this genius are ascribed to the impulse of the Divine Spirit, yet this Spirit and His working are represented in such a manner that their distinction from the natural processes of the human mind becomes a mere assumption, exercising no influence whatever on the interpretation of the phenomenal side of Israel's religion. Writers of this class deal as freely with the facts and teachings of the Bible as the most extreme anti-supranaturalists. But with their evolutionistic treatment of the phenomena they combine the hypothesis of this mystical influence of the Spirit, which they are pleased to call revelation. It is needless to say that revelation of this kind must remain forever inaccessible to objective proof or verification. Whatever can pretend to be scientific in this theory lacks all rapport with the idea of the Supernatural, and whatever there lingers in it of diluted Supernaturalism lacks all scientific character.

I have endeavored to sketch with a few strokes those principles and tendencies by which the study of Biblical Theology is almost exclusively controlled at the present time, because they seem to me to indicate the points which ought to receive special emphasis in the construction of our science on a truly Scriptural and theological basis. The first of these is *the objective character of revelation.* Biblical Theology must insist upon claiming for its object not the thoughts and reflections and speculations of man, but the oracles of God. Whosoever weakens or subjectivizes this fundamental idea of revelation, strikes a blow at the very heart of Theology and Supernatural Christianity, nay, of Theism itself. Every type of Biblical Theology bent upon ignoring or minimizing this supreme, central idea, is a most dangerous product. It is an indisputable fact that all modern views of revelation which are deficient in recognizing its objective character, fit far better into a Pantheistic than into a Theistic theory of the universe. If God be the unconscious background of the world, it is altogether natural that His truth and light should in a mysterious manner loom up from the unexplorable regions that underlie human consciousness, that in His very act of revealing Himself He should be conditioned and entangled and obstructed by man. If, on the other hand, God be conscious and personal, the inference is that in His self-disclosure He will assert and maintain His personality, so as to place His divine thoughts before us with the stamp of divinity upon them, in a truly objective manner. By making revelation, both as to its form and contents, a special object of study, Biblical Theology may be expected to contribute something toward upholding this important conception in its true objectivity, toward more sharply defining it and guarding it from confusion with all heterogeneous ideas.

The second point to be emphasized in our treatment of Biblical Theology is that the historical character of the truth is not in any way antithetical to, but throughout subordinated to, its revealed character. Scriptural truth is not absolute, notwithstanding its historic setting; but the historic setting has been employed by God for the very purpose of revealing the truth, the whole truth, and nothing but the truth. It is not the duty of Biblical Theology to seek first the historic features of the Scriptural ideas, and to think that the absolute character of the truth as revealed of God is something secondary to be added thereunto. The reality of revelation should be the supreme factor by which the historic factor is kept under control. With the greatest variety of historical aspects, there can, nevertheless, be no inconsistencies or contradictions in the Word of God. The student of Biblical Theology is not to hunt for little systems in the Bible that shall be mutually exclusive, or to boast of his skill in detecting such as a mark of high scholarship. What has been remarked above, in regard to the place of individuality in the plan of revelation, may be applied with equal justice to the historic phases through which the progressive delivery of the truth has passed. God has done for the historic unfolding of His word as a whole what He has done for the reproduction of its specific types and aspects through the forming and training of individuals. As

He knew Jeremiah and Paul from the womb, so He knew Israel and prepared Israel for its task. The history of this nation is not a common history; it is *sacred* history in the highest sense of having been specially designed by God to become the human receptacle for the truth from above.

In the third place, Biblical Theology should plant itself squarely upon the truthfulness of the Scriptures as a whole. Revelation proper announces and records the saving deeds of God, but a mere announcement and record is not sufficient to furnish a complete history of redemption, to produce a living image of the new order of things as it is gradually called into existence. No true history can be made by a mere chronicling of events. Only by placing the bare record of the facts in the light of the principles which shape them, and the inner nexus which holds them together, is the work of the chronicler transformed into history. For this reason God has not given us His own interpretation of the great realities of redemption in the form of a chronicle, but in the form of the historical organism of the inspired Scriptures. The direct revelations of God form by far the smaller part of the contents of the Bible. These are but the scattered diamonds woven into the garment of the truth. This garment itself is identical with the Scriptural contents as a whole. And as a whole it has been prepared by the hand of God. The Bible contains, besides the simple record of direct revelations, the further interpretation of these immediate disclosures of God by inspired prophets and apostles. Above all, it contains, if I may so call it, a divine philosophy of the history of redemption and of revelation in general outlines.

And whosoever is convinced in his heart of the inspiration of
the Holy Scriptures and reads his Bible as the Word of God,
cannot, as a student of Biblical Theology, allow himself to
reject this divine philosophy and substitute for it another of
his own making. Our Theology will be Biblical in the full
sense, only when it not merely derives its material from the
Bible, but also accepts at the hands of the Bible the order in
which this material is to be grouped and located. I for one
am not ashamed to say that the teachings of Paul concerning
the historic organism of the Old Testament economy possess
for me greater authority than the reconstructions of the
same by modern scholars, however great their learning and
critical acumen.

Finally, in designating our science as *Biblical Theology*, we
should not fail to enter a protest against the wrong
inferences that may be easily drawn from the use of this
name. The name retains somewhat of the flavor of the
Rationalism which first adopted it. It almost unavoidably
creates an impression as if in the Bible we had the beginning
of the process that later gave us the works of Origen,
Augustine, Thomas Aquinas, Luther, and Calvin. Hence
some do not hesitate to define Biblical Theology as the
History of Dogmatics for Biblical times. To us this sounds as
strange and illogical as if one should compare the stars of the
firmament and their history with the work and history of
astronomy. As the heavens contain the material for
astronomy and the crust of the earth for geology, so the
mighty creation of the Word of God furnishes the material
for Theology in this scientific sense, but *is* no Theology. It is

something infinitely higher than Theology, a world of spiritual realities, into which all true theologians are led by the Spirit of the living God. Only if we take the term Theology in its more primitive and simple meaning, as the practical, historic knowledge of God imparted by revelation and deposited in the Bible, can we justify the use of the now commonly accepted name of our science. As for the scientific elaboration of this God-given material, this must be held to lie beyond the Biblical period. It could only spring up after revelation and the formation of the Scriptures had been completed. The utmost that can be conceded would be that in the Apostolic teaching of the New Testament the first signs of the beginning of this process are discernible. But even that which the Apostles teach is in no sense primarily to be viewed under the aspect of Theology. It is the inspired Word of God before all other things. No theologian would dare to say of his work what Paul said to the Galatians: "But though we or an angel from heaven should preach unto you any gospel other than that which we preached unto you, let him be anathema" (1:8).*

In the foregoing I have endeavored to describe to you the nature and functions of Biblical Theology as a member in the organism of our scientific knowledge of God. I have not forgotten, however, that you have called me to teach this science for the eminently practical purpose of training young men for the ministry of the Gospel. Consequently, I shall not have acquitted myself of my task on this occasion unless you will permit me to point out briefly what are the advantages to be expected from the pursuit of this study in a more practical way.

First of all, Biblical Theology exhibits to the student of the Word the organic structure of the truth therein contained, and its organic growth as the result of revelation. It shows to him that in the Bible there is an organization finer, more complicated, more exquisite than even the texture of muscles and nerves and brain in the human body; that its various parts are interwoven and correlated in the most subtle manner, each sensitive to the impressions received from all the others, perfect in itself, and yet dependent upon the rest, while in them and through them all throbs as a unifying principle the Spirit of God's living truth. If anything, then this is adapted to convince the student that what the Bible places before him is not the chance product of the several human minds that have been engaged in its composition, but the workmanship of none other than God Himself. The organic structure of the truth and the organic development of revelation as portrayed in the Bible bear exactly the same relation to Supernaturalism that the argument from design in nature bears to Theism. Both arguments proceed on precisely analogous lines. If the history of revelation actually is the organic history, full of evidences of design, which the Bible makes it out to be, then it must have been shaped in an altogether unique fashion by the revealing activity of God.

In the second place, Biblical Theology is suited to furnish a most effective antidote to the destructive critical views now prevailing. These modern theories, however much may be asserted to the contrary, *disorganize* the Scriptures. Their chief danger lies, not in affirmations concerning matters of minor importance, concerning errors in historical details, but in the most radical claims upsetting the inner organization of the whole body of truth. We have seen that the course of revelation is most closely identified with the history described in the Bible. Of this history of the Bible, this framework on which the whole structure of revelation rests, the newest criticism asserts that it is falsified and unhistorical for the greater part. All the historical writings of the Old Testament in their present state are tendency-writings. Even where they embody older and more reliable documents, the Deuteronomic and Levitical paste, applied to them in and after the exile, has obliterated the historic reality. Now, if it were known among believing Christians to what an extent these theories disorganize the Bible, their chief spell would be broken; and many would repudiate with horror what they now tolerate or view with indifference. There is no other way of showing this than by placing over against the critical theories the organic history of revelation, as the Bible itself constructs it. As soon as this is done, everybody will be able to see at a glance that the two are mutually subversive. This very thing Biblical Theology endeavors to do. It thus meets the critical assaults, not in a negative way by defending point after point of the citadel, whereby no total effect is produced and the critics are always permitted to reply that they attack merely the outworks, not the central position of the faith; but in the most positive manner, by setting forth what the principle of revelation involves according to the Bible, and how one part of it stands or falls together with all the others. The student of Biblical Theology has the satisfaction of knowing that his treatment of Biblical matters is not prescribed for him exclusively by the tactics of his enemies, and that, while most effectually defending the truth, he at the same time is building the temple of divine knowledge on the positive foundation of the faith.

In the third place, I should mention as a desirable fruit of the study of Biblical Theology, the new life and freshness which it gives to the old truth, showing it in all its historic vividness and reality with the dew of the morning of revelation upon its opening leaves. It is certainly not without significance that God has embodied the contents of revelation, not in a dogmatic system, but in a book of history, the parallel to which in dramatic interest and simple eloquence is nowhere to be found. It is this that makes the Scriptures speak and appeal to and touch the hearts and lead the minds of men captive to the truth everywhere. No one will be able to handle the Word of God more effectually than he to whom the treasure-chambers of its historic meaning have been opened up. It is this that brings the divine truth so near to us, makes it as it were bone of our bone and flesh of our flesh, that humanizes it in the same sense that the highest revelation in Christ was rendered most human by the incarnation. To this historical character of revelation we owe the fullness and variety which enable the Scriptures to mete out new treasures to all ages without

becoming exhausted or even fully explored. A Biblical
Theology imbued with the devout spirit of humble faith in
the revealed Word of God, will enrich the student with all
this wealth of living truth, making him in the highest sense a
householder, bringing forth out of his treasures things new
and old.

Fourthly, Biblical Theology is of the greatest importance
and value for the study of Systematic Theology. It were
useless to deny that it has been often cultivated in a spirit
more or less hostile to the work in which Systematic
Theology is engaged. The very name *Biblical* Theology is
frequently vaunted so as to imply a protest against the
alleged un-Biblical character of Dogmatics. I desire to state
most emphatically here, that there is nothing in the nature
and aims of Biblical Theology to justify such an implication.
For anything pretending to supplant Dogmatics there is no
place in the circle of Christian Theology. All attempts to
show that the doctrines developed and formulated by the
Church have no real foundation in the Bible, stand
themselves without the pale of Theology, inasmuch as they
imply that Christianity is a purely natural phenomenon, and
that the Church has now for nineteen centuries been chasing
her own shadow. Dogmatic Theology is, when rightly
cultivated, as truly a Biblical and as truly an inductive
science as its younger sister. And the latter needs a
constructive principle for arranging her facts as well as the
former. The only difference is, that in the one case this
constructive principle is systematic and logical, whereas in
the other case it is purely historical. In other words,

Systematic Theology endeavors to construct a circle, Biblical Theology seeks to reproduce a line. I do not mean by the use of this figure, that within Biblical Theology there is no grouping of facts at all. The line of which I speak does not represent a monotonous recital of revelation, and does not resemble a string, even though it be conceived of as a string of pearls. The line of revelation is like the stem of those trees that grow in rings. Each successive ring has grown out of the preceding one. But out of the sap and vigor that is in this stem there springs a crown with branches and leaves and flowers and fruit. Such is the true relation between Biblical and Systematic Theology. Dogmatics is the crown which grows out of all the work that Biblical Theology can accomplish. And taught in this spirit of Christian willingness to serve, our science cannot fail to benefit Systematic Theology in more than one respect. It will proclaim the fact, too often forgotten and denied in our days, that true religion cannot dispense with a solid basis of objective knowledge of the truth. There is no better means of silencing the supercilious cant that right believing is of small importance in the matter of religion, than by showing what infinite care our Father in heaven has taken to reveal unto us, in the utmost perfection, the *knowledge* of what He is and does for our salvation. Biblical Theology will also demonstrate that the fundamental doctrines of our faith do not rest, as many would fain believe, on an arbitrary exposition of some isolated proof-texts. It will not so much prove these doctrines, as it will do what is far better than proof—make them grow out organically before our eyes from the stem of revelation. Finally, it will contribute to keep Systematic Theology in living contact with that soil of divine realities from which it must draw all its strength and power to develop beyond what it has already attained.

Let us not forget, however, that as of all theology, so of Biblical Theology, the highest aim cannot lie in man, or in anything that serves the creature. Its most excellent practical use is surely this, that it grants us a new vision of the glory of Him who has made all things to the praise of His own wonderful name. As the Uncreated, the Unchangeable, Eternal God, He lives above the sphere of history. He is the Being and never the Becoming One. And, no doubt, when once this veil of time shall be drawn aside, when we shall see face to face, then also the necessity for viewing His knowledge in the glass of history will cease. But since on our behalf and for our salvation He has condescended to work and speak in the form of time, and thus to make His works and His speech partake of that peculiar glory that attaches to all organic growth, let us also seek to know Him as the One *that is, that was, and that is to come*, in order that no note may be lacking in that psalm of praise to be sung by the Church into which all our Theology must issue.